CLEAN

CLEAN

A New Generation in Recovery Speaks Out

CHRIS BECKMAN

A LARK PRODUCTION

HAZELDEN®

Hazelden
Center City, Minnesota 55012-0176

1-800-328-0094
1-651-213-4590 (Fax)
www.hazelden.org

ISBN-13: 978-1-59285-182-9
ISBN-10: 1-59285-182-7

09   08   07   06   05   6   5   4   3   2

Cover design by David Spohn
Cover photography by Joe McNally
Interior design and typesetting by Kinne Design

This book was written for the people who
need it most—those not yet in recovery.
But I dedicate it to their
family and friends—those who care.

Contents

Contents Other Voices

Contents What You Need to Know

Acknowledgments

I am grateful for everything in my life that has brought me to writing this book, beginning with my amazing family. They've been there for me during the darkest moments, as well as my proudest times. First and foremost, thanks to my mother, Debbie, for her unwavering love and support. And to my little sister, Erin, who keeps me real. And for my father's acceptance and willingness to work on our relationship.

For their generosity and honesty, I thank my friends, especially Pauly, Freddie, Chuck, Sandra, Russell, Ken, and Bruce. Sadly, I must also acknowledge my dear friend Greg, and others like him, who didn't make it. Every day of my recovery honors their memory.

I am indebted to Ginger, who worked with me at Fenway Community Health Center in my early days of recovery, as well as to everyone in the rooms in Boston, Chicago, and New York—particularly my first sponsor, Paul P. Collectively, they showed me how to stay clean and sober. Mike, Tom, and Ed have each helped me dig deeper and move toward an even more satisfying recovery. Their valuable work is much appreciated.

A universal note of gratitude must go to health care professionals around the globe. They are the backbone and foundation for all of us in the first steps of recovery.

I probably would not have made it without a relapse if it hadn't been for MTV's *The Real World,* which I refer to as my halfway house. The producers, Mary Ellis Bunim and Jonathan Murray, directors, and other cast members gave me the space to experience what sobriety was like and the motivation to stay clean. Thank you all.

Thanks to the people who made *Clean* possible. The book would not exist without Robin Dellabough of Lark Productions, who initiated the idea, and Becky Post, my Hazelden editor, who made it a reality. Terence Dougherty, Sarah Verrelli, alumni of Mountainside Foundation in Connecticut, Maggie Keogh, and Dave Hadden of Augsburg College in Minnesota were invaluable in gathering the "Other Voices" stories. Thanks to Lisa DiMona, Karen Watts, and Anna Torres for their editorial contributions and support, and to Joel and Flynn Berry for being inspirational members of a new generation.

Finally, Joe Kelly not only helped me through an often painful writing process but also encouraged and inspired me with his time and wisdom as a fellow traveler. I consider him a true friend.

Introduction

This book is about falling-down drunks and hard-core drug addicts—people just like me. I had my first drink in junior high, and by high school, I was using drugs in a dizzying downward spiral. But I survived as an addict long enough to recover and make it to my real life.

My story has a twist: just after I began my recovery at age twenty-three, I was on the MTV show called, appropriately, *The Real World.* Imagine being constantly filmed while you uncover the confusion, pain, and chaos of how addiction made your life a misery. Then imagine the whole story offered up for public consumption. I had to expose, on national television, my early days of recovery—despite myself. I don't regret that or feel sorry for myself. Temporary embarrassment and vulnerability are nothing compared to celebrating years of living clean and sober.

You don't have to be on a reality show to stop doing drugs. But because of my *Real World* visibility, I've put a familiar face on demonstrating how both addiction *and* recovery can happen, even if you're young.

Today, I speak to college students all over the country about my insane addiction years and my healthy life in recovery, grateful to share my strength and hope. *Clean: A New Generation in Recovery Speaks Out* is my way of reaching an even larger number of kids who struggle with the issues that almost destroyed me.

Despite all the statistics, health class propaganda, lectures, after-school specials, and "say-no-to-drugs" campaigns, a lot of us don't really get the idea that addiction is a disease. I can still remember the colorful pamphlets the school nurse handed out once a year in middle school: educational guides about alcoholism, anorexia, and drug addiction. My friends and I made paper airplanes out of them, telling each other, "This is a joke—are we actually supposed to read this crap?" When any responsible adults talked to me about drugs or alcohol, I just flat-out didn't hear them. I could only hear what my friends told me: the most important thing in life is being cool and accepted, no matter what it takes.

Once I started drinking and using, I still didn't want to hear from anyone that alcohol and other drugs were bad for me. When I was in that destructive addict mind-set, I didn't want any help with the problems my drug use created. I only wanted to pick up more drugs, not some educational guide to recovery. That's why I know better than to tell anyone what to do, whether it is in a book or anywhere else.

So, I won't tell *you* whether or not you have an addiction; there wouldn't be any point. We addicts seem to have our brains wired differently than nonaddicts, with very different thoughts and feelings about alcohol and other drugs. We're blind to the hurt and turmoil our addictions have brought to our lives—and the lives of people we love. That's called *denial,* one of the most stubborn symptoms of addiction. Weave denial into the normal sense of immortality and invincibility that people our age have, and you get a great shot at self-destruction and slow suicide.

Just as I began to write this book, I heard news about a dear friend. Frank was brilliant, he went to Harvard, and he and I used to party together. I hadn't talked to him for quite some time. After three years of witnessing his downhill slide into drugs, alcohol, and serious depression, I finally told him that I could no longer watch him kill himself.

I got sober and he died.

I was shocked but not surprised. Addiction is rampant and has ruined people from every part of my own circle. Two of my uncles died of AIDS as a result of their drug use, and I grew up with a father crippled by alcoholism. These firsthand experiences make the words I hear in Twelve Step groups about "carrying the message to others" hit very close to home. I realize that some people don't ever get to carry the message; like Frank, they have to *be* the darker side of the message.

In the past few years, I've also seen incredible signs of hope as people close to me get into recovery. My father has been trying to stay sober, and we are rebuilding our relationship. A close friend, my former partner, entered recovery—he is the same man who pushed me to get the help I needed to turn the corner.

These experiences remind me every day that in order not to die from addiction, I have to learn to live with it. *How?* is the big question. After all, my generation and the kids younger than me are used to an intense social scene. Going out with friends, which often involves drinking and drugging, feels like the center of our universe. And then we say, "Hey, wait a minute, I'm twenty-one (or fifteen, seventeen, twenty-five, thirty). I just got sober. It's supposed to be like this for the rest of my life? I can't drink like all my friends ever again? I'm giving up so much fun! I have so many unlived years left; I can't imagine doing it without drugs or alcohol."

I talked to myself that way when I first got clean. I remember thinking my whole world had disappeared. Living the rest of my life without drugs felt like being handed a death sentence, and my first reaction was to shout, "Fuck you!" I couldn't experience fun because I didn't know what fun was. I only knew how to get high, drink, and hang out at clubs. When all that changed and getting high was no longer an option, I didn't know what to do other than go to Twelve Step meetings.

Learning to live in recovery as a young person is complex—and sometimes feels nearly impossible. Besides the confusion of the first few months and years of sobriety, we are coping with the upheaval of adolescence, hormones, and growing up. Drugs and alcohol interrupt and stunt our maturation process. We're not rediscovering and reclaiming who we were before we were alcoholics and addicts—because we had not yet become who we would be. We get clean at twenty-three and feel like we're still thirteen emotionally. The crisis that led to our bottoming out turns into an identity crisis as we try to catch up with ourselves and answer the question, "Who exactly am I?"

It's in asking the hard questions that we become aware of a situation, accept it, and act on it. I figure if *Clean* reveals a little bit of what we young addicts learn, accept, and do in recovery, maybe it will help someone else who is in trouble. I also want you to understand what addiction smells and looks like, what it feels like, what addiction leads us to.

I learned that the biggest challenge wasn't necessarily giving up drinking, drugs, and the chemically soaked social scene. It was learning how to live as a person who can connect with other people, be useful, be creative, and have moments of genuine happiness. It was learning how to live life on life's terms.

There is plenty of help along the recovery path for those willing to accept it, but the bottom line is that it takes a moment of turning away from self-destruction and back to self-fulfillment to get on that path in the first place. If you are an addict or an alcoholic, no one can tell you precisely how to have that revelation. They can only describe what it was like for them: how they began to use; the descent into abuse and denial; floundering in the bottom of their disease until finally a split second of grace literally saved their lives.

So, I won't be giving you or anyone else a paint-by-numbers way to recover from drug addiction or alcoholism. Every single person who ever finds a way out from addiction has to make the decision for himself or herself. Fortunately, none of us has to do it alone. That's one of the paradoxes about recovery: we have to make the change as individuals, but we have a lot of friendship and support while we do it.

I'm realistic. I know that not all the people I *most* want to read this book will find it, and that saddens me. Many folks I used to party with are still submerged in the subculture of drugs, clubs, and sex, and of being consumed by useless things. But maybe you're their best friend. Or their mom or dad or sister or brother. I wrote this book for you too.

Maybe these stories of drinking, dropping out of school, abusing drugs, and almost dying can be your example, so you don't have to go through what we went through. I hope *Clean* helps you gain respect for the power of the disease by seeing how drugs got the upper hand with us young addicts.

I'm proud of myself for having the guts to tell my story. In *Clean,* a lot of us get to speak up about staying clean and sober while still enjoying being young. In that sense, this is a support group in book form for us. That is how I, and many addicts, live with addiction and stay in recovery. By sharing our stories, we keep in contact with the memory of our pain. That's how we avoid relapse. By listening to others' stories, we keep in contact with hope. That's how we continue to grow. I am living proof that taking each small but necessary step toward health, freedom, and joy works. No matter how bad addiction is, there *is* always hope.

Note: Except for a handful of public personalities, I have changed the names of the people in this book to protect their privacy. Years of addiction have affected my memory, leaving the details of some incidents cloudy, confused, or forgotten. Please understand that this is my memory of my story, and I am telling it only to show the power of my addiction, not to judge anyone else.

Before the Fall

SETTING THE STAGE FOR ADDICTION

Long before we start drinking or drugging, the demons grow inside, whispering their taunts: you're so stupid, you're so weird, you're so lonely, you're so gay, or, maybe the worst of all, you've been born into a long line of substance abusers. Beware. »

I opened my eyes to find myself on a dirty cot in a cold Boston jail. It was no place for a nineteen-year-old Catholic boy. With a throbbing hangover, I struggled to retrace my last twenty-four hours. But my mind was blank, as though someone had snatched my memory and wouldn't give it back. How could I be here? I was not a criminal! But in the hours that followed, I learned that during an alcoholic blackout the night before, I had assaulted several people, including a cop.

You would think waking up in a jail cell would have made me say, "I have a serious problem with drinking. I need help right away." But I was an addict who hadn't suffered enough yet, and it took me another three years to get the help I needed. On the outside, I was still the all-American Brockton boy. But on the inside, I was falling apart. As it turned out, mornings like this *were* my real world.

THE SPIRAL

I had my first drink, Jim Beam, after baseball practice one afternoon when I was eleven, and from then on I kept drinking. After all, I thought, everyone drinks alcohol, so I must be okay.

7

By high school, I was smoking pot and doing mushrooms. But since these were "natural" plants, not "hard-core" drugs, I figured I was still okay.

In college, I added cocaine, crystal meth, special K, angel dust, ecstasy, and assorted prescription drugs. But as long as I wasn't *shooting up,* I thought, "I'm still okay." By the time I was twenty-two, I was snorting and frantically trying to keep my body filled any way I could with whatever I could get my hands on. I had no more boundaries—if I could've gotten heroin, I would have done it—it didn't matter. I was high all the time, and the only thing I knew was that I *never* felt okay. Hell, I didn't know or care what "okay" even meant anymore.

It didn't make much difference when other people told me I had a problem. Their words didn't even scratch the surface, because I could convince myself that I was functioning fine and that I could get away with being high all the time.

I didn't know it, but I had become completely unreliable in all aspects of my life. Every lie in my life seemed to come crumbling down on me all at once.

So, how does someone go from drowning in the depths of drug addiction to bobbing back up into recovery in a little over ten years? Some people might think ten years of using isn't enough to prove that you're an addict. But people like me know better, even if we are still young.

DEAD END ON TROUT STREET

My story begins with the experience about half our generation has during childhood. When I was about three, my parents divorced. My mother and I lived on a quiet, dead-end Trout Street in Brockton, Massachusetts. It was a secure neighborhood with a mix of apartments, duplexes, and single homes. Down the street was undeveloped land to wander in, and right across from our house was a city park with ball fields. Just a few blocks away was Ziggy's candy store, where my great-grandmother took me when she'd visit.

Mom and I had a two-bedroom apartment in the bottom floor of a duplex. She worked as a bank teller, so after school, a teenage neighbor named Helen came to baby-sit, and I got to be friends with her little brother, Wes. There weren't many kids in the neighborhood, and I didn't reach out much or have many friends.

Still, many of my Trout Street memories are pleasant. I liked being on my own a lot because my imagination and curiosity filled all my time. I remember reading nearly all of Funk and Wagnall's animal encyclopedia, then wandering down the street to collect "data" on our local ecosystem. I was especially fascinated by reptiles. Other times, I did more normal kid stuff, like watching TV, riding my bike, and drawing.

> I couldn't tell the difference between who my father really was and what alcoholism drove him to do (and not do).

My dad lived nearby. He was an active alcoholic who managed to work steadily as a bookbinder. At age six or seven, I began to feel that he didn't want to be around me. I remember Sundays looking out the front window onto Trout Street, waiting for him to come, but he didn't keep his word. Often, all I'd ever see was the empty playground across the street. Over and over, after I had waited for what seemed like forever, my mother would walk in and say that Dad wasn't coming this time.

Being a kid, I couldn't fully understand why my parents weren't together, where my father was, and what drove him to be around or not around. I couldn't tell the difference between who my father really was and what alcoholism drove him to do (and not do). Now I realize that when he missed my Little League games, it might have been because of his drinking, or because my mom sometimes made it difficult for him to see me, or for other reasons I still don't know.

I felt very disappointed and resented losing what I thought a family was supposed to be—the storybook, pristine image of a "true" family with happy kids, a two-car garage, and

Elite Player, Extreme User

MARTHA • FORT WORTH, TEXAS

I'm a recovering addict/alcoholic and a student at Stanford University.

I inflicted terrible pain on my family during my drinking and drug use. But my family was wonderful to me as a child. I was an active, happy kid with lots of friends. I had a fun childhood with everything I needed and most of the things I wanted.

My mom got into AA when I was in second grade, so I don't remember her drinking. I'm happy to say she's still sober today. I was closest to my dad growing up, and my older brother was active in theater and became a child actor.

From an early age, I felt like I had to compete with my brother for the spotlight. So I got good grades, read well, and was outspoken in the classroom. I was constantly told I talked too much, but I had a lot to say to my friends.

I did ballet when young but then quit and started playing sports. It turned out that sports was what I really loved, and I got specifically passionate about soccer. By fourth and fifth grade, I stood out on the soccer field and got recognition for the level of my play.

MARTHA ■ CONTINUES ON PAGE 12

a suburban house with a yard and a dog. That imaginary picture was simple but stable, unlike my real life.

When my father didn't come for his Sunday visitations, I made up dozens of fantasies about the intriguing things I thought he must have found to do. I imagined him living a wonderful, exciting life of romance, adventure—and alcohol. I believed that his incredible life was more attractive to him than spending time with me. I had the sense that my father's absence meant he didn't love me (I was wrong about that), but I also thought it seemed captivating to be an adult who drinks. I chased those feelings of being wanted, and I also tried to find the key to that fantastic, elusive, adult life that alcohol symbolized.

When I was five, my father remarried. I know now that my stepmother, Rachel, is a great person. Today we have a great relationship; she's a riot and wonderful. But back then I resented her a lot. When I was a kid, and all through my drugging years, I never let her into my life because I felt she had unfairly taken my mother's place. Not surprisingly, my mother didn't care for Rachel, and I thought I had to take Mom's side.

On the weekends when my dad and Rachel did show up, they sometimes took me to local bars, including one place called the Charlie Horse that had a kids' arcade—God knows why. My father and my stepmother would let me spend Sunday afternoons at the arcade while they got trashed at the bar.

But there were good memories with Dad too. He loved going to the movies, and we'd go together—he'd let me see horror movies and other R-rated films my mom would never let me see. We'd watch baseball together or go bowling or out to dinner. A couple of times we went fishing at Robbin's Pond. I loved being with him, whenever I could, but those good times were unpredictable and, at least for me, in short supply.

Sometimes he'd take me to visit his side of the family, people I felt I barely knew. I loved my grandparents and their beautiful farmhouse out in Raynham. They had an enormous yard with a river out back. I could get lost wandering around, exploring, and imagining.

When I was with my relatives, there always seemed to be alcohol along with the fun and warm feeling of family. Even when I was little, I remember the excitement of sipping some relative's beer. I think I craved the taste at a very young age, and as I got older, I would sneak down the drinks my relatives didn't finish.

But then it was back to Brockton. When I was ten or eleven, Mom and I moved into another apartment in another suburban neighborhood. There were new places to explore and ride my bike, and I started playing baseball at a nearby field. But still it seemed like I kept to myself, and I certainly felt alone and different.

BINGO CHIPS

Now that I was older, I could stay by myself after school when Mom was at work. I'd sit by my bedroom window and draw and play with my imaginary friend, Freckles, whom I blamed whenever anything went wrong. With my own house key and in charge of my after-school time inside the house, I felt very adult. The feeling was powerful for me because I thought that being an adult would free me from the difficulties and pain that felt central to my childhood. For many years, the desire to be an adult drove the most important actions, thoughts, and decisions of my life.

That was my ticket. Soccer was where I could share the spotlight with my brother.

Even as a kid, much of my drive to be best came from the fact that my self-worth was completely tied up in how well I performed. What I wanted to hear were compliments saying I was a good person, helpful, and the best. I tried never to let anyone see me perform sub-par, because that would bring my confidence down tremendously. I didn't want to be one among many. If not the best, then why bother?

I was competitive, but I was also loyal to and loved my friends. I was outgoing and funny and loved laughing. My friends and I often had sleepovers, and we'd wake up and never run out of things to do. Most of my friends were involved in sports, so after breakfast we'd play basketball. Then we'd have lunch, go out and play soccer, come back in to watch a movie, then go back out to play basketball or neighborhood football. We did this from when we got up until it was too dark to play anymore.

By middle school, I was playing on elite soccer teams. I was sought out by coaches and played on traveling teams and a club team in Dallas, which had the highest level of competition in the state. I went to a private school in Fort Worth, where I also excelled in basketball and cross-country. But soccer was my specialty; I played on the Texas state team, southern regional team, and youth national team. My club team won two state, two regional, and two national titles.

Whenever I played, I focused on standing out. I fed off the recognition. I tried to act as though I wasn't egotistical—at least not out in public. But secretly, I knew I was trying to fill up part of myself with compliments and attention.

I was thirteen or fourteen when I was named to the under-sixteen national soccer team. This was the absolute highest level for a girl my age. I remember standing in the kitchen at home when the phone call came. Instantly, I thought that I was destined for success and that the world had to go my way. It was destiny. I'd be famous and the best.

But within a few seconds, the feeling of excitement had passed right through me; I couldn't hang on to it, and I was on to the next thought. I felt sad and let down, thinking, "What's next? I won't be satisfied until I'm on the U.S. women's national team." It was as if the good feeling of a major accomplishment simply couldn't last inside of me.

I continued to experience this feeling for years. It was like shooting up, getting a rush from compliments and rewards: "You made the team. You won MVP." That would take me up, but then five minutes or five seconds later, or after the trophy was up on my shelf, that was it. The high didn't stick with me, and I'd start searching for what I had to do next to reach the next high. The up and down with my emotions was almost like a drug, and it was rooted in how much fear I had of failure.

So, once I started drinking and using, the pattern was very familiar and the preoccupation with drugs and alcohol took hold right away.

■ MARTHA'S STORY CONTINUES ON PAGE 29 ■

That drive was my way of trying to run away from often-painful present moments, like the days my father didn't show. Creating my own reality was easier than being where I actually was. I remember one time sitting on the dirty, wooden gym floor at St. Edward's Catholic School, counting the colorful bingo chips that lay all around me while wandering off in my head to get through some classroom embarrassment. It seemed like I sat there for an eternity.

Fear and a vivid imagination have always been part of my struggle, starting when I was very young. I was in third grade when, one day after school, I watched a don't-do-drugs program on TV. The show included a "commercial" about lies and lying. The commercial's song played over and over in my head for months afterward. I would sing it repeatedly to myself, at first afraid that telling any lie would ruin my life forever. But eventually, I began mocking the rhyming words and making up bizarre stories about who I was or people I would become or lives I would live.

> As a small child, I developed an inner voice that helped me escape the hard things happening around me.

One life I was forced to lead very young was the life of sexual abuse. When I was eleven, one of our parish priests began sexually molesting me, and he kept doing it for several years. Father was also a family friend, someone my mom relied on often for spiritual support while living the stressful life of a single working mother. His abuse followed the familiar pattern: telling me he loved me, bribing me with treats, and threatening me if I ever told anyone. Later, when I needed moral support, my mom and other relatives encouraged me to turn to the church, and particularly to Father, whom they all thought was my friend and mentor. But that path was closed off by betrayal, fear, and shame. My family never understood why I didn't reach out to Father in my adolescent times of need, and I couldn't tell them.

As a small child, I developed an inner voice that helped me escape the hard things happening around me. But it was a voice that never spoke with or listened to other people, or to reality. This same voice would tell me what was right and wrong or what was honest and fun, and the longer I listened, the more rigid that inner voice got. But on the outside, my life looked—and sometimes felt—like all was okay.

MARTY AND JIM BEAM, MY TWO BEST FRIENDS

By the time I was in junior high, I was playing baseball, and I had my own paper route. I loved making money, so soon I was shoveling snow, raking leaves, and mowing lawns for some paper route customers. I had cash to spend. I had my first girlfriend, and then I had my first drink.

My best friend, Marty, and I were eleven when we sneaked off to the woods near our apartment building with a bottle of Jim Beam. It was a warm, sunny Saturday afternoon, and we had nothing better to do. We just wanted to have some fun. Our relatives who drank seemed to have a good time and drinking let them fit in socially. Marty's father dedicated a whole fridge to alcohol, so there must have been something magical about it. We thought drinking must be something important we had been missing.

Until this point, I'd speculated about alcohol a lot, since I saw so many members of my family use it so often. But that Saturday I got the facts about what liquor could do for me, and I felt like I was tasting history for the first time.

Money, Jim Beam, and girls gave me a taste of adulthood.

Marty and I drank Jim Beam straight out of the bottle. We laughed a lot and got light-headed quickly. Although we were together, I felt very much alone. I can remember a wonderful floating sensation of warmth throughout my body. Not even my mother's voice yelling my name could have interrupted this blissful moment. Time seemed to stand still. In a stupor and naive, Marty and I made a pact to return to the woods after school—or even during school—whenever we could to get drunk.

Money, Jim Beam, and girls gave me a taste of adulthood. I instantly felt like I had become older, wanted, and with it.

THE CHAMELEON YEARS

By seventh grade, drinking made me feel like I was getting laid by high school cheerleaders at senior parties (I wasn't). When I was buzzed, I seemed to become simply strong and sure.

I fell in love with alcohol easily. I learned where my mother stored liquor. Once, I remember drinking most of her bottle of Kahlua and instantly wondering how I would replace it. When I mixed Pepsi in with the remains of the Kahlua, I felt the thrill of getting away with something. But I was also terrified of not being able to talk my way out of the jam if I got caught. Nevertheless, the temptation to drink kept growing, and I began to be bolder about sneaking alcohol at home. One Christmastime, my mother made spiked eggnog. I opened the fridge and drank right out of the shiny porcelain pitcher, then walked around the rest of the day with a slight buzz.

Meanwhile, things at home got complicated. My uncle, a drug addict, landed in jail; of course, that upset the whole family. As I got older, I had to take more responsibility for my little sister because my mother was working three jobs. Eventually Mom had to give up her job at the bank. Money got really tight, and the summer before high school, we moved into the Washburn Heights projects.

What Do Your Parents Do?

JAMIE • WAVERLY, RHODE ISLAND

Both of my parents came from upper-middle-class homes. My father killed himself because he was addicted to heroin and felt that death was the only way to free himself of his addiction.

Immediately following his death, my mother became addicted to crack, marijuana, and alcohol. I spent my childhood living in shacks that were hardly suitable for dogs. In my family, drugs took precedence over food, housing, and all other aspects of normal life.

My childhood and my family were devastated as a result of substance abuse. I can only imagine what it would have been like to grow up with a life, where at school I wouldn't have had to be ashamed or scared when they asked me, "What do your parents do, Jamie?"

Washburn Heights didn't look like big-city high-rise projects. These were small, old, brick townhouses filled with families on welfare. This move was a big shock to my daily routine, but we didn't have much choice.

At school, I was a respectable Catholic boy trying to blend in with the preppy kids. When I got back to the projects, I was a white kid in a mostly Hispanic and black neighborhood. I felt out of place everywhere, and was easily—and sometimes severely—harassed. Then, inside the apartment I was a "grown-up," caring for my toddler sister. I was living a triple life, and it was exhausting and confusing.

I grew up believing that drinking equaled being adult, and being adult was the surest way to leave childhood behind.

I felt afraid of all sorts of things. I was afraid of losing my parents, especially after seeing my uncle die from AIDS due to sharing needles. I was afraid of how I didn't fit in at school or in the neighborhood, and I worried about getting beat up, ostracized, or both.

The desire to escape grew stronger than ever. And alcohol was one easy way out. Once I found a physical substance to grab hold of, I no longer had to keep daydreaming about ways I could flee the present moment; I finally had the means to actually do it! I had the romantic sensation of breaking away from ordinary, dull life.

Now that I had this escape hatch to grab and look forward to, I wanted more and more of it. How beautiful it was to leave feelings behind! It was like I was finally glimpsing how to play the game of adult living and make a big party. Alcohol moved beyond just being a friend. It became the object of my desire.

Drinking seemed like the acceptable and appropriate way to deal with childhood troubles. I grew up believing that drinking equaled being adult, and being adult was the surest way to leave childhood behind. In my extended family and among my parents' friends, adults drank at almost every social gathering. For years I felt left out of that camaraderie because I couldn't drink.

When I first began drinking, I relished many fantasy situations of acting like the adult I knew I'd become when I drank. And when I felt a slight numbness in my legs, I could conquer almost anything. Sometimes I would float or become gigantic—in an electric flash I had superhuman strength. The usual daily mishaps became insignificant and seemed to disappear.

I didn't know how to work my way back and forth between my different lives of school, home, and the projects. But with a drink, my fear and insecurity slipped away. My life felt like it was transforming into one of those beer ads where the hot guy gets the beautiful blonde girl with a tight cutoff T-shirt. As a drinker, I felt I could bask in the wonderful "tastes-great-less-filling" cheers at adult parties and events. I felt like I had a purpose, a belonging, and a newfound friend that was always there, loyal and available.

I did sometimes have a vague sense that drinking was just an anesthetic that numbed, but didn't cure, my deep pain and isolation.

Still, alcohol was acceptable, valuable, and good. At school and at home, I learned that *drugs,* in contrast, were not acceptable; drugs were *bad.* Both of my uncles were addicted to and died because of drugs. Seeing how each of their deaths tore up my family, I swore, "I'll never do that. I'm never going to touch drugs. I'll finish college and live the adult-life fantasy." I didn't see any connection between my drinking (or the drinking of other family members) and the addiction that killed my uncles.

> The truth is, even in the earliest days of drinking,
> I was already conning myself.

The truth is, even in the earliest days of drinking, I was already conning myself. I lied to myself about how much I drank, and I had to lie to my mother and other adults in order to drink. My lying became constant and indiscriminate. I learned to lie about who I was and even made up stories to try to fit into, or stand out from, whatever situation I was in.

I could change colors as quickly as my pet chameleon, Peppy, one minute hiding behind a good-Catholic-schoolboy shirt and tie, and the next minute playing and dressing the part of a tough, smart-ass punk from the projects. No one could tell me what to do and the Catholic school rules didn't apply. Compulsive lying flowed most easily in the warm glow of being drunk.

Drinking and lying to myself and others weren't yet my constant companions every moment of every day. But they got worse as I grew older. In fact, even on my best days, I felt separate, isolated, and not present with the people and situations around me.

For example, at many family events, my body was present, but not my mind. Instead of joining in the love of my relatives, I visualized how I wanted my life to be or how I wanted my family to fit society's ideal. Over time, living in a world of fantasy, lying, and escape, my perception of "right," "wrong," and "reality" morphed into something my mother and the nuns at St. Edward's wouldn't recognize.

LASHING OUT IN THE CLOSET

My internal struggle with what other people thought was right and wrong reached its peak early in high school when I could no longer kid myself about my sexuality. I knew I was gay, but I remained strictly closeted because I was so fearful of other people's reactions—and because I was so afraid of fully admitting I was gay. I dealt with the confusion by being one of the most homophobic guys at my all-male high school during the day and by sneaking off to the park for oral sex with strangers at night.

When I was a junior, everyone started labeling a freshman named Jeff a homosexual. I was one of the leaders. One time on the bus to school, I grabbed his tie, called him a fag, and spit on him. My behavior was alcoholically intense, and I suddenly felt enraged at Jeff. I saw a look of real fear in his eyes. Afterward, I felt like I'd humiliated myself, as well as him, and I got drunk to drown the embarrassment.

A Teenager's Tears of Hope

JANE • ONTARIO, CANADA

I'm an alcoholic, and I'm fifteen years old. I was raised in an alcoholic home. I had my very first drink when I was eleven years old. I hated it—the taste, the smell, everything. So, I didn't drink right away. But the year I was fourteen, I wanted to be independent, you know, to take charge and be carefree. And I wanted to be cool. At first, it seemed harmless to have five beers, feel kind of tipsy, and laugh a lot. You see, I had a horrible past, having been molested from the time I was age five to age ten by my own relatives, and then by my older brothers until I was eleven years old. Soon I wasn't drinking once or twice a month; it was every weekend.

That summer, I got a job and a boyfriend who didn't drink. The relationship lasted a month. I lost my boyfriend because I ended up making out with a guy who was twice my age at a party (and who was put into the hospital that morning by my friends). But hey, who cared? I had money, I had friends who were cool, and I was finally cool.

Most weekends were a haze: I'd go to a party, drink, have a good time, and come Sunday, go home, usually with the cops, but not always, and have a great story to tell for days. The things I usually left out were waking up in strange places half-naked, puking all over myself, and finding mysterious bruises and scrapes on my body in the weirdest places.

Soon fall came, and I was a grade behind, but I didn't care as long as I partied on weekends and had a good time. No problems, no worries, no harm done. That's what I thought, until one day when I went to the bathroom. My groin area was itchy, and I noticed an awful smell and a burning sensation. I never told anyone. I studied some information about sexually-transmitted diseases and read in horror the signs and symptoms of genital herpes. I looked at my body—the bumps on my groin area, the bumps on my lips, the discharge in my underwear. I cried for the longest hours of my life when I read that it was incurable. I still had not gone to see a doctor after nine months. Why? Because I was scared of rejection, of dying, of losing all my friends and family.

Guess what came to the rescue? Alcohol and, this time, drugs. I started to drink anything, anytime, anywhere, with anybody.

■ JANE'S STORY CONTINUES ON PAGE 87 ■

19

I pointed the finger at Jeff, a gay kid, because he was everything I was interested in being. He did drama and artwork without apology. He was flamboyant and didn't talk to many other boys. I wanted to be friends with him even while I harassed him. But I was too insecure; I was afraid what other people at school would say about me if I started hanging around with Jeff or boys like him.

I didn't want other people to think I was gay, even though part of me already knew that I was at least bisexual. I was desperately trying to search out a physical way to be who I was, but I couldn't seem to find it. I projected my own self-hatred onto Jeff, but I wanted to be close to him too. Perversely, the harassment gave me a way of being in contact with him. According to the rules in my head and among my peers, the only way I could touch him was to hit him.

Even during the days and weeks I didn't drink, I craved the warm glow alcohol provided and had a lingering hunger for the next escape.

I hid behind those beatings because I was filled with guilt and shame whenever I felt attracted to other boys or men. I was Catholic and going to a Catholic school. But my church didn't seem to have a place for any gays. If I were to sum up everything I learned from the church about being gay, it would boil down to this: homosexuality is a disease of manhood. I didn't want to have a disease, but I knew I was gay. And so I picked on kids like Jeff and drew as much attention as I could to how gay they were.

But most of all, I just wanted to get through high school and everything else associated with being "a child" as soon as I could. Then, I thought, I could live and drink on my own, and I could come out as gay and be who I truly was.

Meantime, drinking could get me high, let me become anyone, and "free" me from the pain of staying in the closet, being poor, having parents who weren't married anymore, feeling like an undeserving outsider, and having a childhood that wasn't as perfect as I wanted it to be.

Even during the days and weeks I didn't drink, I craved the warm glow alcohol provided and had a lingering hunger for the next escape. I was clearly obsessed already, even though I couldn't drink all the time because I was so young and lived at home with my mother.

All of these feelings and thoughts caused me to be alone in my head even in the safest of social settings. I never stopped examining how or why I felt so different from normal kids. But when drunk, I became very pleased with my compulsive thoughts and my "unique" take on everyone and everything else. In a pattern that would plague the rest of my addiction, I began daily plotting for my next taste of Jim Beam freedom.

COMING OF AGE IN MONTREAL

On a sudden impulse, I took my first trip to Montreal for a drinking holiday at age eighteen. I felt the rush of legally and openly ordering a drink. I felt the luxury of coming of age— to have the freedom to go where I wanted and get what I wanted.

When those Montreal bartenders made me a drink, I felt like I was near to attaining something I'd always missed out on before. It was important to reach for and have this feeling because it would justify or liberate me.

Reading this, you may get the impression that my family's drinking and drugging wrecked my life or predetermined my life as an addict. That is simply not true. Sure, my parents' actions sometimes hurt me, but they also healed and nourished me. I'm not different from any other human being when it comes to that.

Divorce, a parent who drinks, a parent who smokes, blended families—none of these things make a kid (or an adult) into an alcoholic or drug addict. Genetics plays a role in addiction, but genes aren't responsible all by themselves. Nor is environment. Some alcoholics grew up in families where no one ever drank or where people drank only occasionally. Some people who grew up in ragingly addicted families never develop a single drug or alcohol problem.

I'm not sure you can ever really figure out what "causes" me or anyone else to become an addict any more than you can, with absolute certainty, figure out what causes someone else to become a diabetic. What matters is what we do about an addiction problem. Does the addict stop using and learn how to handle life's problems with a clear head? Does the diabetic watch his diet and faithfully take his insulin? Answer those questions, and the what-causes-it question becomes irrelevant.

Addicts can't even see that the drugs are the problem . . . it looks to us like everything else besides drugs—and everyone else besides us—is the problem.

Unfortunately, I went many more years before I started dealing with my addiction, or even realized that addiction was the central question in my life. Instead, I followed the path of most addicts and alcoholics before me, no matter how old they were when they started or stopped. I continued to disappear into isolation, drowning the pain and resentment, and ultimately making drugs and alcohol into—far and away—the most important relationship of my life.

To anyone with a nonaddict's mind, it's obvious that turning an inanimate substance into the most meaningful object of your affection is the way to ruin a life, not a way to run a life. But when caught in the desperate whirlpool of addiction, up looks like down. Addicts can't even see that the drugs are the problem. Instead, as you'll read in the next chapter, it looks to us like everything else besides drugs— and everyone else besides us—is the problem. That's because denial is ruling our lives.

Risk Factors
WHAT YOU NEED TO KNOW

Genetics

Whether or not you can "inherit" substance abuse has been debated for decades. The most recent studies say genetics accounts for 40 to 60 percent of the risk for developing substance abuse. You don't actually inherit alcoholism itself—you inherit the brain chemistry that makes you more vulnerable to it. Not only do children of alcoholics have chemical imbalances that make them prone to substance-abusing behaviors, they respond physically to alcohol differently than children without the genetic predisposition. So, for example, if you have a parent or another biological relative who is an alcoholic, you are more likely to feel a heightened sense of pleasure or elation and relaxation after drinking alcohol than someone who does not have alcoholism in her family. If you and a friend from a nonalcoholic family have identical blood alcohol levels, your friend would feel the effects of the alcohol sooner than you.

Having a family history of alcoholism does not guarantee that you will become an alcoholic, but your chances of repeating the pattern are increased. Studies show that dysfunctional family dynamics, feelings of shame or alienation, and other psychological factors common to families where alcohol plays a part may also increase your risk for substance abuse. This holds true in spite of your awareness of family history, even after saying to yourself that you won't be another link in the alcoholism chain (see Your Family below). It is important that you understand these risks as you lead your life in recovery. If you have your own children someday, don't forget to let them know that they are at risk as well.

Your Family

Your family's social or economic status does not appear to be a risk factor for chemical dependency. Along with a genetic predisposition, however, your family dynamics may contribute to alcohol or substance abuse. According to the Medical Council on Alcoholism, any of the following factors may increase the risk of psychological and social problems in kids—whether they are the children of alcoholics or not. These social and psychological problems, in turn, may increase the risk of alcohol or substance abuse.

Specific stressors:
- parents' alcoholism
- death of a parent
- parents' unemployment
- parents' divorce or separation
- illness of a parent

Family relationship issues:
- Can you depend on family members?
- Is the family unhappy?
- Do family members understand you? If not, do they at least try to?

Communication problems in the family:
- Do family members talk about problems directly or only hint at them?
- Do family members show affection?

Conflict in the family:
- Do family members criticize each other?
- Fight a lot?
- Ignore each other?

Mental Illness and Emotional Problems

Mental illness and emotional problems definitely increase the risk for alcoholism, substance abuse, smoking, and other forms of addiction. If you suffer from depression or anxiety, for example, it's common to try to self-medicate with alcohol or other substances. People who are uncomfortable in social settings may turn to alcohol or other substances in order to become less self-conscious in public.

Because alcoholism itself may cause chemical changes in the brain that *produce* anxiety and depression, it is not always possible to know whether a person with emotional problems is using alcohol to self-medicate or whether the alcohol itself is causing emotional disorders. But it has been shown that drinking less alcohol can improve the emotional state of moderate drinkers, so knowing the connection between mental illness and substance abuse is helpful as you move into recovery. Depression in users may also contribute to more instances of relapse.

If you have emotional problems or depression, your treatment might include the use of antidepressants such as Prozac, Zoloft, Paxil, Celexa, and Luvox. Drugs like these act on the level of serotonin (a neurotransmitter in the brain that regulates the effects of alcohol) and may actually reduce the desire for alcohol. Antidepressant medication may also reduce cravings for alcohol even in people who are not depressed. Ask your doctor whether or not these antidepressants, or newer classes of drugs that target neurotransmitters other than serotonin, may help in your recovery.

Note: If you have a dual diagnosis—substance abuse and mental illness—your treatment is going to be more complicated. The more serious the mental disorder, the more likely it is you may feel a compulsion to use. If you have mental illness, get help from medical professionals. You will need a comprehensive treatment plan in addition to any self-help programs, such as Twelve Step programs, that focus only on addiction. ■

2

Drunk and Stoned

BECOMING CHEMICALLY DEPENDENT

Some kids can pick up a beer at a party, drink it, put the can down, and get on with their lives. For the rest of us, from the minute we take that first sip, drinking *becomes* our lives. »

While I denied my sexuality throughout high school, there was no pretending that alcohol had not changed my life forever. At first, drinking opened a door to a new way of experiencing life. It seemed to free me to be different at an age when nearly everyone is terrified to be labeled as different. It helped me overcome the fear that, if I were gay, people wouldn't accept me or accept who I thought I was. I ran scared from the feelings I knew I had for men—but a few drinks made all the confusion easier to take. Drinking made me feel more comfortable in my own skin.

For most addicts, our drug of choice often works fairly well in the very beginning. It soothes our upsets, numbs our pain, covers up our shame, and seems to slay our inhibitions. Who wouldn't want something that does all that, and tastes good too? Because we're addicts, we keep medicating ourselves and end up denying that it's our fault when we crash and burn. That means we lie to ourselves and to people around us, especially the people who show us the most love and affection.

SCAMMING SISTER VERA

Addiction isn't just about using alcohol or other drugs. It's also about using other people, manipulating them and stringing them along to get something without having to earn it.

25

Sister Vera was my creative writing teacher in high school and a very sweet, kind, and loving adult in my life. She was small and, even though she didn't wear a habit, she looked just like a nun. I used to think that if Sister Vera were a food, she'd be Quaker Oats—natural, pure, and good for you. I was drawn to her nurturing ways.

She introduced me to great poems, and I fell in love with e e cummings, reading his words aloud with fun and passion. So, when my art teacher had us make a sculpture that represented a favorite poem, I chose one of cummings's that starts "i thank You God for most this amazing / day: for the leaping greenly spirits of trees." Thinking about the poem, I tried to express the emotion of a man embracing life. The sculpture looked a bit like those cheap, cheesy, pudgy, little statues a high school girlfriend would give you—with big, goofy eyes and the message "I love you!" across the bottom. My papier-mâché version, with his head fallen a bit over to one side, reached his arms out wide to hold close the joy and love of other men.

A few days later, Sister Vera stopped me in the hall and said how much she'd enjoyed seeing it on display. "I love your portrayal of Christ in your sculpture, Chris!" she said. "It is so clever how you show him on the cross, but without the cross visible behind."

I would scam even the people who were the best to me if it meant I could avoid some consequence I didn't want to face.

By this point in the semester, I was drinking and drugging a lot and wasn't doing very well in Sister Vera's class. Without missing a beat, I started to suck up and lie. I said, "That's really great, Sister; you're the *only* one who saw what I was trying to do! I'm so glad you figured it out. That makes me feel like I really accomplished something!"

Right away, I knew I had scored. Sister Vera was so pleased that she glowed, and then she started heaping more praise on my artistic ability. Meanwhile, I was feeling invincible. I had completely scammed her, and she didn't have a clue. Inside, I was strutting, thinking, "Hey, man, I got this bitch around my little finger." I was immensely proud, and I felt even more satisfied with myself when Sister Vera gave me a decent grade for the semester—one that I didn't deserve.

And this was how I treated someone I had a great relationship with. I would scam even the people who were the best to me if it meant I could avoid some consequence I didn't want to face, like a bad grade for goofing off.

> I felt I had no outlet to talk honestly with anyone about much of anything important to me: my drinking, the gay sex, my childhood history, and so on.

Of course, the biggest lie was dating girls while craving sex with men. I was about sixteen the first time I had sex with a guy. I went up to a park where I knew gay men gathered for casual sex. I was scared shitless, but even more, I wanted to experience that freeing sex with another man. I followed a stranger walking his dog into the woods. There was a warm breeze, and as we walked under the green trees, he asked me to help him find the lake. There was no lake in that park, and I started to freak out, thinking I'd be raped or killed. I imagined seeing my dead body in the woods, but worse was the fear of people knowing I was there—getting caught among the gay guys. Despite my paranoia, I kept going and the man gave me oral sex. It was physically thrilling, but at the same time, I wanted to shove him away because I was scared; I liked it too much, and I wanted to fight how much pleasure I felt.

When it was over, I went to my car and drove from there straight back to my girlfriend's house. It was easy to go to her, easy to lie to her, easy to make up stories of where I'd been. This only reinforced my shameful pattern of lying to people who cared about me—and whom I cared about. But I felt I had no outlet to talk honestly with anyone about much of anything important to me: my drinking, the gay sex, my childhood history, and so on. Instead, I kept on acting and feeling as if I were living a triple life.

Let me be clear—my struggle with my sexuality didn't make me an alcoholic/addict. The more accurate view is that the way I manipulated other people in sexual and romantic relationships was a glaring part of my addiction. The classic book on addiction, *Alcoholics Anonymous,* says that addicts are the personification of "self-will run riot." It goes on to say that most alcoholics have been regularly selfish, dishonest, and inconsiderate in their sexual relations, sowing jealousy, bitterness, and suspicion in their wake. About alcoholic sexual behavior, the book says: "Many of us needed an overhaul there."

The fact that I am gay didn't keep me from trying to use female friends in high school to fill my emotional neediness. That felt great to me. I didn't have to return the favor, and these girls were almost always fun to be around. I was good-looking, and it was a plus for them to be seen with me.

I thought I would marry my first real girlfriend, Susan, because she really seemed to love me for who I was. Susan was very open, and her family—even her dad—liked me. We dated on and off for about a year. We talked, hugged, and kissed romantically, but we never had sex. Even then, I felt like deep inside me a seedling was splitting in two. My life looked like it was growing a "straight" seedling, but another seedling was taking off toward the light of my emerging sexuality.

CHEATING

The same thing was happening with my drinking. At school, at church, and with my family, I played a role of being straight, as in clean and sober. I went all out in the role of good, responsible Catholic boy who didn't do those nasty drugs so many adults were worried about. I was sneaking drinks at home and getting drunk every other weekend (more and more frequently), but people didn't seem to notice.

I thought I was getting away with my act, putting on a show of the handsome, steady, happy teenager. I was painting a beautiful picture of myself on the outside for public consumption. But inside, I felt as if I were falling apart as I juggled my roles and continued the cycle of lying to my

Elite Player, Extreme User

MARTHA • FORT WORTH, TEXAS

■ MARTHA'S STORY CONTINUES FROM PAGE 12 ■

I had my first drink at a New Year's Eve party during my freshman year of high school. It was some horrible concoction of liquors with Diet Coke. It radiated fumes of poison and smelled terrible. I could tell it was gonna burn my insides. But I knew before I put my lips to the cup that I was about to partake in a sacred ritual. I don't know how I knew, but I did.

The drink tasted wretched. But I drank it anyway because I'd seen other people drink and knew it helped them drop their inhibitions. I wanted to be transformed. I didn't get drunk, but I was more affectionate than normal toward my boyfriend, and I felt more a part of the party. I wanted attention and thought everything I said was funny. I started to feel better with the warm feeling that crept inside my veins.

Before long, I was drinking regularly and wasn't interested in friends who didn't use. I dropped some friends I could be really honest and present with. Irritability and restlessness crept into every day, and I started to feel trapped in the boring and mundane unless I was traveling with one of my teams, winning championships, or drinking. I was very moody and in a completely flat emotional state most of the time.

I smoked my first pot at a concert with a friend, but I couldn't get high. I kept smoking and smoking, but it wasn't altering my perceptions quick enough. I'd take a hit and look around hoping to see things differently or to start laughing. I was looking to get out of my mind, and it wasn't working. I was furious but couldn't show it. If my friend saw me cursing at not being high, that would be strange; smoking dope, I should be mellow, not uptight. Who wants to see someone else get angry? I was angry because I was still sober.

Eventually I was able to get high, and I started using pot a lot. My bedroom was upstairs, so I'd smoke at night and blow it out the window. I smoked before school and driving home too. I wondered, "How do people get up and do life sober? Why would they?" I had already crossed the imaginary line and I wasn't gonna be able to go back. I already was able to excuse my using and ignore conscious warnings or intuitions telling me that this was out of control. Why did I drink and get wasted when the state championship was the next day? I rationalized things like this as "mistakes." I'd say to myself, "That's partying for you; stuff just happens. What I did is no sign of alcoholism; I shouldn't be branded as a lush. Everyone parties and someone's gonna get sick." It was usually me.

I drank most weekends and soon planned my week around getting drunk. Already in high school, I was possessive of alcohol. Once I was out driving with some girlfriends, and one of them had a fake ID. She said, "I'll get a case of beer for everyone, okay?" I panicked and thought, "What if someone drinks more than their share and I don't get enough?" So I said, "A bottle of vodka and a six-pack for me, please." My friends asked, "Why do you need a bottle of vodka and a six-pack? Why not split the case with us?"

MARTHA ■ CONTINUES ON PAGE 31

friends about who I was—and lying to my family about my drinking and our family priest. Whenever I could sneak out for a drink, I'd run from being the good Catholic boy to doing my best to drown and numb my pain and confusion in liquor. All the lying meant I got away with some insane behavior— and it turned out that I was good at that.

For example, I got to be best friends with Hillary in part because her family had the stability and warmth that I didn't feel in my own family. Watching her parents was a vicarious thrill for me. Not only did they seem perfect—they were still together. Hillary's house was a good, safe place to be. I'd charm her parents and flatter her brother by talking art with him.

Early on, I realized that Hillary was in love with me, and I used that knowledge to my advantage throughout our whole relationship, without ever reciprocating the feeling. I'd win her over whenever there was a window of opportunity. If I needed her to do my homework for me, I'd bat my eyes or offer to help her clean the house, and she'd always do it. In situations like that, I went in with a mission and came out with what I wanted, even from the people I loved best. I really thought I was a good friend (and sometimes I was). I also knew that I had become a person who used other people and that I was warped in some way that frightened me—but not badly enough to make me stop.

Whenever I could sneak out for a drink, I'd run from being the good Catholic boy to doing my best to drown and numb my pain and confusion in liquor.

Another benefit of hanging around at Hillary's was how it helped me with my mother. Mom knew that Hillary had a strong Catholic family, and she trusted that I'd be safe and well cared for while I was there. I'd tell Mom I was going to Hillary's but then go out and drink instead. I might stop by Hillary's for a bit before or after, but basically, when it came to Mom, Hillary and her family provided me a pretty foolproof cover for my drinking.

They didn't know I wanted to take that bottle home. What if the girl with the fake ID wasn't with us next time we went out? At least this way I had alcohol. I always asked for more than my share to keep a stash.

I had a science to it, already planning my night out by what levels to drink and when. For example, a few shots of vodka would give me a buzz so I could space it out and not get drunk too quick, get sick, and embarrass myself. That made it possible to then have some beers later. Mostly, I hated to depend on others for my alcohol or other drugs. I needed direct contact with my dealer and my own fake ID. I wanted to get it when I wanted it.

Meanwhile, I was being recruited for soccer by major colleges all over the country. In my senior year, I committed to Stanford on a full soccer scholarship—another thing that filled me up with momentary excitement and then passed.

Earlier in high school, I had gotten up before school to go train at the gym. I'd run, go home, shower, and then head to school. I was health conscious in my eating. And I dismissed my weekend drinking because I thought, "I can bounce back easily when I'm young." Halfway through my junior year, smoking more pot late at night, I rationalized not working out anymore: "It's crazy to get up at 5:30 in the morning anyway; no one does that! I certainly don't need to because I can stay fit without training. Besides, aren't big-time schools knocking on my door already?"

I looked to do the minimal amount of training and schoolwork that I could get away with. When my mom asked why I didn't train anymore, I told her I simply didn't have time to get up that early. But the real reason was smoking pot at night; I couldn't get up anymore and was starting to get lazy. I couldn't admit that it was related to pot.

I once saw the world as exciting, with destiny going my way. Now I saw it as really boring. I felt sick of how mundane everything was. I felt flat, blah, and drab unless something dramatic happened. By drinking and using, I could control my reality, thoughts, and feelings. That's why I loved and became preoccupied with weekends. Friday morning, I was thinking about Friday night. I was no longer living in the present or even thinking about the short-term future.

I went to a party the night before one of our state championship games, getting so drunk that I was lying on the bathroom floor sick when I got home. Dad came in to wake me and he could tell—there was a trash can beside the bed. The room was spinning and I didn't know how I'd get up and play. I threw up when I got out of bed and felt terrifically hung over. Out at the field before the game, I threw up again. But I played the game and we won. I threw up afterward, after holding it in on the field. To me, that was the end of that. I could play it off. That whole episode just meant I could get away with it but needed to be smarter next time. We won, I played well, and I thought no one knew what made me sick.

MARTHA ■ CONTINUES ON PAGE 33

31

As I look back, I think I wanted my alcoholism to take over. Living the life of a Catholic schoolboy, I had a master plan to get into good Catholic girls' homes, scam their parents, eat food from their fridges, and get wasted with them on the weekends. And I did it. Whenever Hillary's parents were gone, I'd arrange to hang out at her house so we could spend time together drinking. We made friends with kids at a nearby college who could buy us liquor, and I'd show up there at five and stay until ten listening to music, eating, and drinking. Then I'd leave and go use with a friend before going home. Plus, it all looked good to my mother, because I was spending so much time at a nice Catholic girl's house!

USING DENISE

Hillary's best friend was a girl named Denise, and I was very jealous of the bond they seemed to have. From the first time I met Denise, I set out to ingratiate myself with her—in part because she didn't seem to like me.

I had just gotten my driver's license, and Hillary asked me to pick up Denise at a friend's. Right away, I started plotting how to make a best-ever impression on her. Wanting to show off, I cleaned out the car and cued up the CD player to be blaring the Breeders' song "Cannonball." I was sure the fact that I was onto such a cool group would convince her that I was cool too.

When Denise got in the car, I eagerly asked her if she liked the Breeders, and she just rolled her eyes at me as if I were a complete dork. I felt kicked in the gut and shocked that my usually reliable methods seemed to be failing. I then felt completely determined to get her to like me.

It was just like the way I played my divorced parents off against each other.

Meanwhile, I still envied Denise's friendship with Hillary, and I wanted what they had. I worked hard to become friends with each of them separately from the other and then play the two off against each other. I'd tell Hillary, "So, you know what Denise said about you last night?" and vice

In my senior year, I started using 'shrooms. And then I tried cocaine during a lunch break. I immediately thought, "I never wanna run out of this stuff." I was absolutely in love with it. I felt like it was a beautiful, sunny day with the windows open; I felt so high and energized. I didn't feel mundane anymore. And I thought, "This is something you can do all the time without anyone noticing! Coke doesn't make your eyes red; you don't smell of booze; this is perfect!"

The rest of my friends did coke every once in a while. Right away, I was asking the girl who gave it to me where she got it—but trying not to let her see how urgent it was. I said, "I want some more because I have other friends who are interested in trying it." But it was really all for me. My coke use quickly got more progressive. I did it in the bathroom at home. At Christmastime, I was doing it around the family, thinking that I was leaving no signs of trouble along the way.

In February, I came home from a basketball game to find my parents had my bags packed. A friend of mine had just gotten busted, and my parents found out I'd been trying to buy speed from him the week before. They shipped me off across the state for three months to the first of what turned out to be numerous drug treatment programs.

The Stanford coach found out I was in treatment, and he could have pulled my scholarship. I called him when I got out and he was understanding, promising to keep the scholarship in place and to help me when I got to campus.

But when I left treatment later in my senior year, I started drinking, using, sneaking, and lying again. Now when my parents confronted me about using, my attitude was: "No addict or alcoholic gets into a school like Stanford on a full scholarship. No addict or alcoholic does things that I do, like being on elite traveling teams and winning championships." I was convinced that I didn't fit the stereotype.

■ MARTHA'S STORY CONTINUES ON PAGE 55 ■

versa. It was just like the way I played my divorced parents off against each other. The whole time I was undermining their friendship, I remained convinced that I was very fond of both girls and was doing what was best for them.

Ultimately, I succeeded in getting Denise away from Hillary, and I made her more loyal to me. Denise said she wanted to lose her virginity before leaving high school, and so I played sexual games with her to string her along and to make Hillary more jealous. I made Denise think that she'd be with me someday, toying with her emotions shamelessly, especially when I was drunk. I regularly conned her into buying me dinner or covering for me so I could go drink—I even convinced her to throw a party for me in Boston.

I was always looking for what I could gain by holding her an emotional hostage.

Denise's family wasn't as together as Hillary's seemed to be. I could sense that Denise was needy and I took advantage of that. I was always looking for what I could gain by holding her an emotional hostage.

When I started dating yet another girl, Andrea, Denise wrote me a long, heartfelt letter telling how much she loved me and wanted me for herself. She wrote how jealous she was and complained about what a whore I was. She described all the good things, sexual and otherwise, she could do for me better than Andrea could. She pleaded with me to understand how special we were and what her love for me meant to her. She spun romantic visions of how we could be together, madly in love. Finally, she told me how deeply hurt she was by how I was using her.

I responded by playing games with the letter. About a week later, Andrea and I were out by the reservoir, drinking with a group of people from where I worked. Denise drove up and tried to join in. But I didn't want her there. I wanted to keep this drinking crowd as a separate part of my life, without her in it.

So, with Andrea on my arm, I walked up to Denise and

started making crude allusions to the letter she'd written—comments that no one else but her would understand. She'd signed her letter "D-Girl," and in a condescending, sarcastic voice, I started saying, "Hey, D-Girl! How ya doin'? Still in love with that boy, D-Girl?" Only Denise knew what I was referring to, and she knew I was spitting venom at her. Then I sneered at her and said, "Hey, D-Girl, wanna stay for a beer?"

After I completely humiliated her, Denise stomped off in tears. I was taken aback by how obviously (and easily) I had hurt her. So I set right off to find *myself* a beer to start drowning my guilt. I got really smashed that night. But the guilt didn't stop me from continuing to play with Denise's emotions. Later, when the two of us were alone, and no one else was around to judge, I opened up to her again and regained her trust.

SMOKING POT

Buy things for me. Hang around until I need you. Disappear when it's inconvenient for me to have you around. Lie for me. This is how I treated my friends. Maybe I learned to manipulate so effectively from the priest who had used the same methods on me. Wherever it came from, I was a quick study on getting people to do things I wanted them to do, even when they didn't want to do it. Believe it or not, a part of me knew what I was doing was wrong and hurtful—but another part of me felt smug and happy that I was getting away with it so well.

> Hanging around and smoking pot felt like it could help me fit in with the project kids. I wanted to feel accepted and do what everyone else was doing.

I first crossed paths with marijuana when I was twelve and a kid in my neighborhood tried to sell me a joint. I was deathly afraid of trying it and self-righteously thought I'd never stoop to using drugs—even though I was already using the drug of alcohol. But once I was fourteen and living in the projects, I hung out with a crowd that smoked and sold pot. I'd get high a lot at Logan's place because his

Good Catholic Girl
DANIELLE • MORAGA, CALIFORNIA

I was part of the campus ministry team at my Catholic high school. Although at first there weren't clear divisions, near the end of the year, there was a split growing between the people who partied together on the weekends and those who didn't. I was one of those who didn't.

I smoked pot for the first time the summer before my freshman year at St. Mary's College, and I got drunk a total of two times that same summer. I thought, "Well, that's what you do in college, might as well get an early start." When I got to college, I sneaked off to smoke with another freshman girl while the rest of our class was doing some icebreakers. We happily gallivanted off to talk about theater, *The Sound of Music,* and my trying to play the pennywhistle; she became my best friend. Her roommate was some chick from Bakersfield, a punk/raver who had been in rehab a few times for speed. Then there was a bona fide raver from Pasadena who raved about the prospect of getting some K.

Before I went to college, the most I had heard about drugs was a little about E, weed, and alcohol. I did drugs and alcohol for about a year, from the first day of my freshman year in college. The first two weeks, I was sober for two days, and the rest of the time I was drunk. At the end of two months, I had dropped E a few times, dropped acid a couple times, drank more alcohol than I can remember, played around with Ritalin, smoked weed pretty regularly, had fun with the thirty-second nitrous high, tried some prescription antidepressants and sedatives, retched because of 'shrooms, and learned how to smoke at least half a pack of cigarettes a day. I guess I wanted to experiment.

mother was hardly ever home, and he got away with murder. Hanging around and smoking pot felt like it could help me fit in with the project kids. I wanted to feel accepted and do what everyone else was doing.

Soon I was smoking at school too, waiting around after class to buy a joint. I started out using pot once or twice a month, then it was once or twice a week, and then—all the time. At first, I didn't like how pot slowed me down and made me stupid. But I did like the sense of belonging I felt, being on the same trip with everyone else, laughing together, eating the same food, and listening to the same music. There seemed to be camaraderie in getting high and in the lifestyle surrounding it.

Not long after I started, I'd moved from smoking my friends' pot to getting my own bags to a dime habit. With my addict's mind, I started thinking and plotting about how I could do pot without having to pay for it. Often I could convince friends to let me smoke for free. Then I started dealing myself. I'd buy an ounce, sell three-quarters of it, and smoke the rest.

I also discovered some girls whose fathers were dealers —and I made sure I dated those girls. After school, I'd blow off the bus and walk with a girl named Ashley to her house, where she'd go into her dad's room and pull a tin can from his closet, and we'd smoke for free. I forgot what I'd tell my mom while I was off getting high. By this time, I was sometimes high in front of her, although she didn't know it.

> At first, I didn't like how pot slowed me down and made me stupid. But I did like the sense of belonging I felt, being on the same trip with everyone else.

I liked the instant escape, and some days pot seemed easier to manage than alcohol. I stopped playing baseball and didn't do much homework (I could con friends into doing it for me!). But I kept on working—mowing lawns, shoveling snow, and, at fifteen, getting a job at McDonald's—so I'd have money to drink and smoke pot. I saved some money so I could eventually get away from home.

Living like this, I spent a lot of time covering my tracks and planning my escape routes when I got caught. I used ridiculous excuses for what I was doing: "I'm out of uniform because I left my shirt in the back of my car." "I didn't do my homework because I was sick." "I missed school because my cousin died." "I was late for class because I got in a car accident." Of course, with such lame excuses, I got caught a lot and sent to detention for this stuff, as well as for fighting and talking back to teachers.

Looking back, I see that partying always got first priority. I did the minimum at school so that I could get people off my back and free myself up to get high or drunk.

It was difficult to manage work, school, and partying. Looking back, I see that partying always got first priority. I did the minimum at school so that I could get people off my back and free myself up to get high or drunk. I went to work high sometimes, and I would give my friends free food in exchange for a promise that they'd let me get high later.

On Saturdays during my senior year, when I wasn't working, I'd go to the park to play basketball and get high. It was an excuse to be out all day, and I needed excuses. I was one of the few kids with a mother who tried to keep track of her children, so I had to have alibis. I lied to her so I could hang out with kids she didn't approve of. The lies kept her off my back and protected my fake reputation as a good boy in the family.

It was just as important to maintain my reputation among friends too. To cover my tracks at home and at the basketball courts, I'd lie to the boys about where I was headed. I'd say, "Gotta go now. I'm going over to a girl's house to get laid," when where I was really going was home to stay out of trouble with my mom. If I told them how different my mother was, they'd call me a mama's boy and not accept me.

Partying and covering my tracks was a lot easier when I turned sixteen and got a car. I still lied to my mom about where I was after school and on weekends, but it took less effort to pull off the scams. Because my mother trusted

Hillary's family, I'd tell her I was at Hillary's house in the afternoon working on a school project, when I was actually over at Ashley's getting high. I also jumped from girl to girl to find the ones with the best access to pot and alcohol, no matter how much it hurt the feelings of my closest female friends. All that mattered was getting high and drunk.

WHAT'S THE USE?

I always thought of myself as honest and loyal, but I was breaking down those boundaries in search of my drugs—a pattern that continued for years. I used dope and made excuses daily, developing a craving for that instant escape.

At the start, I loved the sensations of cloudiness and warm feelings of glowing and numbness that pot provided. Music and TV sounded different when I was high. At the beginning, the pot-induced hallucinations seemed new and different each time. There was an instant, uplifting release and immediate rush, as if I were passing through the center of my mind to the center of my being. It felt like a spiritual experience of floating in reality and like my artistic mind could take over and create.

But in reality, my artistic mind never did get down to the dirty work of actually creating anything while I was high. My life slowed down and my motivation to accomplish things faded away. I didn't want to do any schoolwork or get up on Saturdays to go to work. I had short-term memory loss and couldn't keep my concentration to draw or paint.

Smoking dope was more than a new hobby; it was my whole life. It made me feel super-attractive and wanted. I could loosen up and become funny, cool, and different from the normal kids and the normal me. I felt as if I were living life on the edge of "mom control." It was an exciting, fun game to get away with everything. But I remained an outsider and looked like a dope to many of the other kids and adults I admired. After all, when your biggest thrill in life is fooling your mother or principal with a lame excuse, you're not really living much of a life.

I didn't see things that way at the time. All I cared about was using. Brockton winters were bleak, so that was a reason to get high and drunk. Summers made it easy to get away from home, so that was a reason to get high and drunk. Spring and fall were filled with school, which I wanted to escape, so that was a reason to get high and drunk.

As a freshman I avoided the "smoking table" where kids gathered outside after school, sure that I'd never take up that nasty habit—but before long, I was joining in. I started smoking pot before school with the guys everyone knew were the biggest potheads. One time I brought an alcohol concoction to school in a Mountain Dew bottle and drank it throughout the day. As an upperclassman, I could sign myself out of a last-period study hall, which I did often to go and get stoned. I'd hang out after school or drop friends off at their houses on my way home, smoking pot the whole way. Then, when I got home, I'd tell my mother I'd stayed late to work on a class project.

Throughout all these years, I still had a very loving and accepting mother. Mom was capable of giving me the emotional support I needed—and willing to do it.

Eventually, I got a job at a Friendly's restaurant where I could get high with little hassle. The manager got stoned regularly, and my dealer would drop pot off there for me. I got Logan a job there too. When we worked the same shifts, we'd get high beforehand and stay stoned all through work. I had the chance to do other drugs, but I didn't. I was afraid to do acid because Logan had once had a bad mescaline trip. But mostly, I didn't feel the need to do harder drugs because alcohol and pot were still working fine for me.

Throughout all these years, I still had a very loving and accepting mother. Mom was capable of giving me the emotional support I needed—and willing to do it. The problem was I didn't want to accept it from her. I was also unwilling to accept the difficult feelings that I had, and so I ran from them and from her and my sister. Living with them became a burden to me. When I was younger, alcohol had represented the wonder and excitement of adulthood. Now, moving out of the house became incredibly urgent, so that I could be released to achieve that drug-laden adult life I so wanted. Moving out would free me up to date men, do what I wanted, and drink without limits.

In fact, it would "free" me to be chained in addiction to still more drugs.

The Substances

WHAT YOU NEED TO KNOW

Alcohol

Common short-term effects:

- Giddiness, talkativeness
- Intoxication
- Slurred speech
- Drowsiness

Possible short-term effects:

- Loss of self-control
- Nausea, vomiting
- Light-headedness
- Increased blood pressure and heart rate
- Memory lapses
- Blurred vision
- For very heavy users, blackouts
- Loss of coordination

Possible long-term effects:

- Alcohol dependency/addiction
- Weakened immune system
- Weight gain
- Weakened bones
- Liver cancer or cirrhosis
- Brain damage

Alcohol affects the brain, as well as the circulatory, nervous, and reproductive systems, causing changes in sleep, attention, memory, coordination, and judgment. Alcohol is produced by fermenting fruits, vegetables, or grains.

Several factors contribute to the effect alcohol has on an individual. These include how quickly the alcohol is drunk, how much food is in the drinker's stomach, family drinking history, and the drinker's body weight, expectations, emotional state, drinking environment, and gender. Safe alcohol use for most adults is no more than two drinks a day for men and one drink a day for women and older people. (One drink equals one 12-ounce bottle of beer, one 5-ounce glass of wine, or 1.5 ounces of 80-proof distilled spirits.) Binge drinking means more than five drinks at one occasion. Drunk with a meal, alcohol will be absorbed, which can reduce the blood alcohol concentration by half. The legal drinking age varies from state to state, but a breath test can be failed after only one drink.

Alcohol affects the outer layer of the brain (the frontal cortex, which regulates conscious thought) most directly. Other cells vulnerable to alcohol are those associated with memory, attention, sleep, coordination, and judgment. Alcohol causes the loss of inhibition. It impairs memory by preventing the transfer of information in long-term memory. Even small amounts of alcohol can inhibit REM sleep, making one tired on awakening.

Those who use alcohol heavily for years may suffer permanent brain damage, changes in personality, and memory loss. Men may suffer lowered testosterone levels, breast enlargement, testicular shrinkage, and impotence; women may undergo menstrual irregularities, infertility, and loss of libido. Years of usage weaken the body and cause many health problems, including chronic high blood pressure, deterioration of the heart muscle, anemia, and stomach ulcers. Alcohol also contributes to the development of cancers of the lip, mouth, throat, larynx, stomach, intestines, and liver.

Cocaine

Common short-term effects:

- An immediate rush
- Euphoria
- Feeling of mental alertness
- Decreased need for food and sleep
- Dilated pupils
- Constricted blood vessels
- Increased temperature, heart rate, and blood pressure
- Anxiety, irritability
- Sexual arousal

Possible short-term effects:

- With larger doses, violent or erratic behavior
- Tremors
- Vertigo
- Muscle twitches
- Hallucinations
- Paranoia

- Respiratory failure
- Cardiac arrest
- Seizure
- Sudden death

Possible long-term effects:

- Addiction
- Paranoia
- Auditory hallucinations
- Irritability, restlessness
- Paranoid psychosis
- Loss of interest in sex
- Heart attack or chaotic heart rhythms
- Coma
- Chest pain, respiratory failure
- Stroke
- Abdominal pain
- Nausea
- Weight loss or malnourishment
- Effects of regularly snorting cocaine: loss of sense of smell, nosebleeds, problems with swallowing, hoarseness, chronically inflamed septum and runny nose
- Effects of regularly ingesting cocaine: severe bowel gangrene due to reduced blood flow
- Effects of regularly injecting cocaine: puncture scars ("tracks") in forearms, allergic reaction, death

Cocaine hydrochloride is a highly addictive, naturally occurring drug extracted from the coca plant. Called crack or freebase cocaine in its refined state, it powerfully stimulates the central nervous system.

Street names include coke, C, snow, flake, junk, nose candy, candycaine, rock, basuco, and blow. It is usually sold in a fine, white crystalline powder, generally diluted with substances such as sugar, cornstarch, or talcum powder, or cut with other stimulants such as amphetamines. Freebasing is a method that prepares cocaine to be smoked— never injected—by eliminating the hydrochloride to "free" the cocaine base itself. Crack is a less concentrated form of freebase cocaine, made using baking soda rather than ammonia and ether. Its name comes from the crackling sound it makes when smoked.

Cocaine is taken through the mouth ("chewing"), the nose ("snorting"), and intravenously ("mainlining" or "injecting"). In its freebase form, it is only smoked in a pipe or as a cigarette. When cocaine powder is snorted, it is absorbed into the bloodstream through the nasal tissue. Injection and inhalation produce the most rapid, heightened effect, because the drug is released or absorbed directly into the bloodstream.

Cocaine achieves its effects by stimulating the region of the brain that produces pleasurable feelings. A part of the neural system called the ventral tegmental area (VTA), located deep within the brain, appears to be targeted most directly. Nerve cells originating in the VTA extend to the brain region called the nucleus accumbens, which involves all types of pleasure, including food, water, sex, and other drugs. Cocaine causes a buildup of dopamine in the brain, which continuously stimulates neuron receptors, resulting in euphoria. Its effects begin ten seconds after a dose and last between a few minutes and a few hours. Maternal use of cocaine during pregnancy may harm the fetus and cause the child to be born prematurely, underweight, or shorter than average. Cocaine users, especially those who inject, are at increased risk for HIV, hepatitis C, and other infectious diseases.

Ecstasy

Common short-term effects:
- Sensation of euphoria or lightness
- Higher alertness
- Increased sensitivity to touch, taste, smell, and light
- Blurred vision
- Chills/sweating
- Distorted experience of time
- Warped perceptions
- Significantly increased heart rate and blood pressure

Possible short-term effects:
- Sleep disturbances
- Depression
- Nausea
- Hyperthermia
- Hallucinations

Possible long-term effects:
- May affect memory and ability to learn
- Paranoia
- Long-term brain damage (among heavy users)
- Can damage the serotonin system, which regulates sexual activity, aggression, and sensitivity to pain

Ecstasy is a laboratory-made drug, popularized in nightclubs and raves in the 1980s. Chemically similar to the stimulant amphetamine and the hallucinogen mescaline, ecstasy itself is nonaddictive, but it is often cut with addictive substances. Dealers often dilute the expensive tablets with cheaper, more dangerous drugs, and it can be difficult to determine if an ecstasy pill actually contains ecstasy or how much. Initially prevalent within the rave scene, where it fueled all-night techno dance parties, ecstasy later spread to urban streets. Some people consider it a "gateway drug," one taken by first-time drug users who later become hooked on addictive substances.

Street names include MDMA, XTC, X, E, rolls, white doves, mitsubishi, and other "brand" names. Among the more expensive of club drugs, it is sold only in pill or tablet form for about $20 to $25 each, as of this writing. The conditions under which this drug is taken greatly influence users' experiences. Ecstasy can cause severe dehydration and hyperthermia, sometimes exacerbated by the hot and crowded club environment. In some cases, users drink excessive amounts of water to counteract rapid dehydration, causing "water intoxication" (hyponatremia). This potentially fatal condition dramatically decreases electrolytes. Ecstasy can also affect the hormone that regulates the amount of sodium in blood; low levels of sodium can result in hyponatremia. Its effects typically last four to six hours, though some users report anxiety and sleeplessness that continue for days or even weeks.

Because the substance has been used recreationally for only two decades, little research on the long-term effects of ecstasy has been done.

Studies on animals suggest that chronic use can cause long-term brain damage in the serotonin system, which regulates sleep, sexual activity, and moods, among other functions. High levels of this drug in the body sometimes result in liver, kidney, and cardiovascular system failure. Deaths associated with ecstasy use frequently result from dehydration or heart failure.

Heroin

Common short-term effects:
• Surge of euphoria ("rush")
• Warm flushing of skin
• Dry mouth
• Alternating feelings of alertness and drowsiness (being "on the nod")
• Clouded mental functioning

Possible short-term effects:
• Fatal overdose
• Severe itching feeling
• Sensation of heaviness in hands and feet
• Suppression of pain
• Changes in respiration

Possible long-term effects:
• Fatal overdose
• Addiction itself
• Spontaneous abortion
• Infection of the heart lining and valves
• Abscesses or other soft-tissue infection
• Cellulitis
• Liver disease
• Pulmonary complications such as pneumonia

- Drug may also contain insoluble additives that clog blood vessels leading to the lungs, liver, kidneys, or brain
- Collapsed veins
- Arthritis
- In cases of intravenous injection, risk of infectious diseases such as HIV and hepatitis

Heroin is a highly addictive drug processed from the substance morphine, found in the seedpod of some poppy plants. It is the most frequently abused and most rapidly acting of the opiate drugs, taking effect eight seconds after intravenous injection. U.S. heroin use has increased 35 percent since 1995.

Street names include smack, H, junk, and skag. Heroin is sold as a white or dark powder, usually cut with other substances such as quinine, sugar, or powdered milk, and sometimes with the poison strychnine. Most commonly injected intravenously, it can also be smoked or snorted. It takes effect rapidly by entering the brain, where it is converted to morphine and binds to natural opioid receptors. Tolerance develops with regular use, and the addict must use more heroin to achieve the same intensity of effect. After tolerance is raised, addiction and physical dependence develop because the body has adapted to the drug's presence; withdrawal symptoms may occur if use is reduced or stopped. In regular users, withdrawal symptoms may occur as soon as a few hours after the last administration, peak between forty-eight and seventy-two hours later, and largely subside after a week. For heavy users in poor health, sudden withdrawal is occasionally fatal. Unintended withdrawal may occur because users cannot be sure of the drug's potency or actual contents. HIV and other infectious diseases can be transmitted by sharing injection needles.

Longtime heroin users also face severe withdrawal symptoms. These include restlessness, cravings, bone and muscle pain, diarrhea and vomiting, kicking or other muscle spasms, cold flashes with goose bumps ("cold turkey"), and death.

Marijuana

Common short-term effects:
- Giddiness, euphoria
- Muscle and breathing relaxation
- Increased heart rate

Possible short-term effects:
- Nausea
- Hazy, slow thinking, drowsiness
- Dilated pupils
- Intensified latent fears
- Strong, sudden appetite ("the munchies")
- Disorientation
- Impaired ability to recall events
- Impaired judgment

Possible long-term effects:
- Breathing problems
- May affect ability to learn
- Lowers testosterone levels temporarily
- May affect male and female reproductive systems and fetuses during pregnancy
- Higher risk of lung cancer for heavy users

Marijuana is a mixture of the crushed leaves, seeds, and flowers of the hemp plant. Stronger forms of marijuana include sinsemilla, hashish, and hash oil. Marijuana is one of the most commonly used drugs: 25 to 50 percent of high school seniors in the United States are current users.

There are hundreds of street names for marijuana. The most common include pot, weed, herb, grass, ganja, skunk, dope, reefer, spliff, and fugazi. It is usually smoked like a cigarette (called a joint) or in a hookah, water pipe, or bong. It can also be baked in brownies or boiled for a weak tea.

Marijuana's active ingredient, THC (delta-9-tetrahydrocannabinol), quickly travels throughout the body and to the brain. There it attaches to cannabinoid receptors on nerve cells that regulate movement, coordination, learning, memory, and functions such as judgment and pleasure. Marijuana also alters the user's brain chemistry by inhibiting the function of the neurotransmitter acetylcholine, a chemical that transfers information from one nerve cell to another. A high usually lasts fewer than three hours, depending on the potency of the drug.

Marijuana is nonaddictive. It may affect the reproductive system of men and women because reproductive cells absorb more THC than other body cells. The drug can also cross the placenta, affecting a fetus during pregnancy. Marijuana somewhat reduces testosterone production, but hormone levels return to normal after a user quits smoking.

Mescaline

Common short-term effects:
- Feelings of mind expansion or ego dissolution
- Vivid, intense, and colorful hallucinations
- Restlessness
- Synesthesia (merging of the senses)
- Confusion of colors
- A lucid mental state, heightened awareness
- Bodily relaxation or tranquility
- Dilated pupils
- Escalated blood pressure and heart rate
- Warmth
- Loss of coordination or balance

Possible short-term effects:
- Stomach weakness or vomiting soon after ingestion
- Nausea
- Feelings of being overwhelmed or scared
- Fear that the trip will not end
- Loss of appetite
- Difficulty breathing
- Taking the drug while depressed or anxious may result in a bad trip
- Functions as an aphrodisiac

Possible long-term effects (scientific research is inconclusive about some chemical specifics):
- No known withdrawal symptoms
- Psychological dependence
- Disinterest in reality
- Flashbacks
- Latent psychoses may be triggered by the drug

- Increased risk of developing schizophrenia later in life among very heavy users
- In extreme cases, abusers may experience hallucinogen persisting perception disorder (HPPD). This disorder involves vision disturbances (trailing images, spots, and auras) and depression/panic attacks that persist long after use, sometimes permanently.

Mescaline is a naturally occurring hallucinogen found in several cactus species, but it is also produced artificially in illegal laboratories. Synthetic or pure crystalline mescaline is one of the rarest psychedelics, but many counterfeit substances are sold under the name mescaline. Mescaline is about four times as potent as ecstasy and lasts more than twice as long.

Street names include cactus, mescal, moon, topi, and bad seed. Mescaline is most commonly extracted from peyote, a small, spineless cactus that grows in the southwestern United States. Its flesh is harvested in the summer, cut in slices or "buttons," and dried or stored indefinitely. The buttons are usually softened and then eaten, but they can also be powdered, made into capsules, liquefied, boiled for tea, smoked, or injected intravenously. It may take a week or longer to fully recover from a mescaline high, which itself lasts around twelve to fourteen hours. Tolerance develops within three to six days, and users of other hallucinogens may find that they have a high cross-tolerance for mescaline.

Mescaline stimulates the brain, causing visual hallucinations. The drug interferes with the neurotransmitters dopamine and norepinephrine due to the similarity between their chemical structures.

Mescaline produced in illegal labs for underground consumption sells at $100 to $200 a gram ($50 to $100 a dose). Its high cost is one reason it's not as widespread as other psychedelic drugs. Peyote possession or consumption is unlawful for all but members of the Native American Church of North America. Harm is usually not done by the drug itself, but from the user's loss of coordination while under its influence. Overdosing is rare; but if mescaline has been combined with other drugs such as barbiturates, the risk is increased.

Methamphetamine

Common short-term effects:
- Decreased need for sleep
- Diminished appetite
- More activity
- Greater attention
- "Rush" or euphoria
- Irritability
- Rapid breathing
- Increased heart rate
- Dilated pupils
- High blood pressure
- Higher body temperature

Possible short-term effects:
- Hyperthermia
- Confusion
- Convulsions
- Anxiety
- Aggressiveness
- Cardiovascular collapse/death

Possible long-term effects:

- Psychosis (usually temporary, sometimes permanent) including visual or auditory hallucinations, paranoia, delusions, extreme mood swings, repetitive motor activity
- Insomnia
- Extreme weight loss
- Stroke (irreversible damage to blood vessels in the brain)

Methamphetamine is considered more addictive than alcohol or heroin, and it is one of the hardest substances to kick. A chemical related to amphetamine and produced in illegal laboratories, methamphetamine has more powerful addictive and stimulating effects on the central nervous system.

Street names include speed and meth. A form of methamphetamine hydrochloride that looks like ice crystals is called ice, crystal, glass, and tina. Besides these crystals, it comes in chunks, tablets, capsules, or powder and can be white, off-white, or yellow. Users smoke, snort, swallow, or inject methamphetamine, depending on its form. Ice, for example, is smoked in a glass pipe like crack cocaine. The odorless smoke leaves a residue that can be resmoked. Smoking meth can affect a user for twelve hours or longer.

Methamphetamine releases high levels of the neurotransmitter dopamine, which results in elevated mood and agitated body movement. Long-term research has proven that methamphetamine can damage neurons containing dopamine and serotonin. Using methamphetamine seems to shorten the neurons' nerve endings, or terminals. These terminals don't die completely, but they don't grow back either. Eventually, methamphetamine use reduces the natural levels of dopamine in the brain by as much as 50 percent and serotonin by an unknown amount. The toxic effects include a serious movement disorder similar to Parkinson's disease, depression, and psychosis.

Chronic abuse can lead to psychotic behavior—paranoia, visual and auditory hallucinations, out-of-control rages, violent behavior, and, occasionally, homicidal or suicidal thoughts. An addict who stops taking the drug may experience depression, anxiety, fatigue, paranoia, aggression, and an intense craving for the drug.

Special K

Common short-term effects:

- Hallucinations, intensified colors and sounds
- Dreamlike state or delirium
- Amnesia
- Loss of coordination
- High blood pressure
- Depression
- Out-of-body or near-death experience
- Numbness
- Slurred speech
- Exaggerated sense of strength
- Aphrodisiac

Possible short-term effects:

- Potentially fatal respiratory failure
- Coma
- Sense of invulnerability
- Muscle rigidity
- Aggressive or violent behavior

- Blank stare
- Oxygen starvation to brain and muscles
- In large doses, convulsions or vomiting

Possible long-term effects:
- Physical or emotional dependency
- Coma
- Death

Special K is a street name for ketamine hydrochloride, a nonbarbiturate anesthetic mainly used as an animal tranquilizer by veterinarians. It is legal for medicinal use only.

Other street names for ketamine include K, vitamin K, kit kat, and kathy. Ketamine highs are sometimes called K-holes, black holes, or K-land. Ketamine itself is a liquid, injected intravenously or intramuscularly for the most potent effect, although there is a risk of losing motor control before completing injection. It can also be made into a tablet or powder resembling cocaine to be ingested, smoked, or snorted. It is sometimes mistakenly sold as ecstasy or mixed with other drugs such as ephedrine or caffeine.

Special K is chemically similar to PCP (angel dust). Because it is an anesthetic, if a user harms herself under its influence, she may be unaware of the injury. Its effects usually last an hour, but may continue four to six hours and take the user twenty-four to forty-eight hours to fully recover. The effects of chronic use require several months to two years to entirely wear off, and flashbacks may occur even a full year after use. ■

3

Believe What You Want

DENIAL COMES ON STRONG

By the time we black out, get arrested, are almost killed, or almost kill someone else, we know we have a problem. But that is almost never the same time that we stop using. We are very good at forgetting. Addicts learn to lie, and they lie best to themselves. It's a default setting called denial, a survival technique for the addiction itself. »

I always wanted to be an artist, and today I am living my dream as a painter in New York. But it hurts to look at the images I painted during my drugging years. One painting was an aerial view of a massive rushing river. The river is dark and confused with no beginning and no end. Because I painted from an overhead perspective, the painting itself has no horizon line. I think I painted that way because my life had no horizons then, either. Looking back, I can see that the painting was an accurate reflection of my life; I didn't know where it might end and I was afraid to look at or imagine it. In many ways, my life was becoming as scattered and chaotic as a Jackson Pollock painting.

STUDIO NIGHTS

Within a month after graduating high school, I moved out of my mother's house and into an apartment that Hillary's grandparents owned in the Hyde Park neighborhood of Boston—with Hillary as my roommate. I was thrilled about the place because it had beautiful wood floors and an attic. Right away, I began creating big plans for converting the attic into my studio so I could finally throw myself into painting. I saw fabulous potential in the space, and the gay man in me was released to decorate.

I told all my friends that I was learning carpentry and drywall so I could clean up and paint the attic. I told grand stories of the handyman skills I was mastering, the supplies I'd bought, how I'd do the remodeling, and how much work it was going to be. I lied and told people I'd just been to Home Depot to buy sheetrock.

The truth was I never set foot inside a lumberyard. But I absolutely *knew* I would eventually! Meanwhile, while I kept building the attic studio in my mind, I never actually started doing any of the work. That attic would have made a fantastic studio had I followed through with my plans. Instead, it turned into a party room where I'd pass out face down on the floor from drinking.

This kind of behavior may sound ridiculous, outrageous, and absurd. To tell you the truth, I laugh at myself when I remember some of these stories.

During one of our first parties, Hillary was drinking beer when I bumped into her bottle. The force of my hitting the bottle broke her front tooth in half. Hillary cried out in pain, and then, when she looked in the mirror, she sobbed, "I'm never going to be pretty now!" Rather than apologizing or being there to comfort her, I laughed in her face. Because I was drunk, I found the whole episode hilarious.

I remember another night my friend Pete peed on the floor up there, thinking it was the bathroom. He did it right in front of me—I was furious about how he was ruining my new studio! I grabbed Pete and started shaking him, belligerently shouting, "What the fuck are you doing pissing all over my beautiful walls? I'm gonna put sheetrock right there; are you crazy?"

This kind of behavior may sound ridiculous, outrageous, and absurd. To tell you the truth, I laugh at myself when I remember some of these stories. But the behavior is also so typical of the denial and delusion central to an addict/alcoholic's thinking—my own included.

INDEPENDENT LIVING

Moving out of my mother's house was liberating and painful. Dishonesty was creeping into every aspect of my life. I hid my packing and kept threatening to move, but I didn't tell my family I was actually going until a couple of weeks before I left. That whole period was hypertense, and in the end, I felt I was jilting them. I remember that summer day, knowing that my sister and mom didn't want me to go. Mom definitely thought I wasn't ready to live on my own. But I felt sure that freedom was on the other side of that door; I had to move on because there was an unknown world to explore.

My eight-year-old sister stood there crying, pleading with me not to go. The look in my mother's eyes hinted that she felt the same way my sister did. She said, "I love you, Chris," while my sister turned to her and wailed, "Why does he have to go?" I was startled by their reaction and could see the pain on their faces. I was only moving thirty minutes away, so why all the fuss? Witnessing my behavior over the last few years, maybe they sensed that I was cutting loose the last anchor I had to sanity—my family—and was about to lose myself on a very dark voyage. If so, they were right.

> Knowing I would be living on my own, I had already begun planning the parties and drinking.

But I told myself that the move would bring me to a better place with more independence. And I'd be closer to Suffolk University in Boston, where I planned to start college in the fall. (They had given me a scholarship based on financial need.) I was confident that my life had a greater purpose. I had every intention of doing right by school, getting educated, and then becoming someone responsible with a job and family.

My first apartment held incredible power for me. Getting it seemed like perfect timing and meant I didn't have to be in a dorm. Knowing I would be living on my own, I had already begun planning the parties and drinking. It would be easier because, on my own in a big city, I could be anonymous and not have to check in with or make excuses to anyone.

This was the big step into the holy ground of adulthood, something I longed for all my life. I could live on my own, buy cigarettes, and get drafted. Of course, I resented that it was still against the law to buy liquor, but I could easily get someone to buy enough to stock my fridge. Plus I now had a sure place to have parties. According to the rules and score sheet in my head, the discipline and responsibility of paying bills gave me the authority to drink and do as I pleased. We addicts have a thousand rules in our heads that allow us to justify selfish behavior while simultaneously setting us up to regularly feel bad about ourselves.

This was the big step into the holy ground of adulthood, something I longed for all my life.

Living off campus, I felt like an outsider when I started at Suffolk. I arranged my schedule to have classes only two days a week, and the rest of my time was dedicated to partying and to working enough to pay my bills, buy alcohol, and buy drugs. Within a month, partying rose to the top priority. School quickly became nothing more than a chore, like having to sweep the apartment floors every week—and I hate housework.

I resented school, stopped doing homework, and began to work full-time. My first real job was working at a community health clinic for gays and lesbians. I still presented myself as straight, but I got trained as a peer educator on HIV/AIDS issues. Work didn't bother me because it gave me a sense of authority, and I had more money than I'd ever had before. I started to skip classes with Hillary so we could go drink. Every weekend, we'd have friends over to party. I could see that things were getting out of hand with school, and I tried at first to get it together and in order, but I couldn't handle it.

Meanwhile, given my self-imposed pressure to succeed

and fulfill my parents' expectations, my failure made me feel guilty. I wanted to do what needed to be done to become the person I wanted to be, but I was also fearful and paralyzed by the pressure of providing for myself and my addiction. Even though I'd finally crossed over into living like an adult, inside I felt just as lost as a teenager trying to fit in at school. All this led me down the path of drinking even more. Getting drunk and high was the easiest getaway, and it seemed to relieve the pressure. It helped me put stuff out of my mind. It relaxed me and I felt like it gave new purpose to life. I wanted nothing as much as I wanted to continue touching that freedom and tasting that warm, if temporary, comfort.

DIFFERENT PERSON TO DIFFERENT PEOPLE

At the health clinic, I met gay people I liked, including the first guy I could imagine myself staying attracted to for longer than a one-night stand. Nothing came of it, but the experience opened my eyes to the idea of a potential emotional commitment with another man, a big step beyond the merely physical release of gay sex I'd had up to then.

The clinic was my first experience with people tolerant and accepting of homosexuality; so I felt a strong need to come to terms at least with being bisexual. I came out as bi to Hillary, who was totally cool with it. That gave me courage to overcome some of my

Elite Player, Extreme User
MARTHA • FORT WORTH, TEXAS

MARTHA'S STORY CONTINUES
FROM PAGE 33

■

I thought leaving for Stanford would be my saving grace. I could start new, away from my nagging parents. Because my mom was sober in a Twelve Step program, I thought she was trying to label me alcoholic. Once I got away from home, I'd get out from under her thumb and I could prove I wasn't.

As soon as I got to California, I was drinking and drugging just like I did in Texas. I got drunk and smoked pot daily. I went to class sometimes, doing just enough to get by. During soccer practice in the afternoon, I'd think, "I've got work to do; can't get drunk tonight; don't have time." But I knew once I picked up one drink, drinking would be what I did for the whole evening. The minute someone asked me to smoke pot, all bets were off. All promises were off. I was sure there was nothing wrong with one hit, but it always turned into several, and I'd be unable to function or do work the rest of the night. Instead, I'd just be hanging out in a daze with my using friends.

MARTHA ■ CONTINUES ON PAGE 57

55

fears and come out to my mom. It was hard to tell any other human being, let alone my mother, because I struggled with the shame that came from being homophobic, raised Catholic, and feeling like I was sinning. I felt I was letting down my religion, and letting down what I *thought* my mother wanted me to be—a "normal," happily married man.

Mom was startled, but also more open, loving, and accepting than I had expected. She asked, "Are you safe? Have you been tested for AIDS?" She suggested that I talk to the family priest for guidance and support. That suggestion hurt me a lot, but she didn't know why, and I couldn't tell her about his abuse. It was clear she was struggling to work it all out, so I tried to ease our joint discomfort by saying, "It's probably just a phase I have to experiment with. Don't worry, you'll have grandchildren someday." But her reaction showed me clearly that she loved me for who I was, no matter what. Today my mother is the most accepting and wonderful force in my life.

No amount of apparent support from family and friends was enough to stop my addictive slide.

Then I started coming out with some straight male friends, who were also very supportive. But soon I abandoned them, certain that they'd no longer feel comfortable hanging around with me at night because I'd be a threat to them. None of them ever said such a thing, or apparently even thought it, but I was convinced and burned those bridges behind me. The truth is they did care for me as a friend—the situation was all about me, not them; all about me not loving myself. I decided it was easier to become a different person to people who didn't know me than to do the work of being honest with people who cared about me— and who might catch on to how much I was now abusing drugs and alcohol. No amount of apparent support from family and friends was enough to stop my addictive slide.

Years later, after I'd reestablished a strained relationship with my father, I came out to him. I was afraid to do it, but

As things got worse through my daily use, I rarely called home. I didn't understand why my roommate called home every week and kept in touch with her family. I never thought to call, and I couldn't talk on the phone after 6:00 at night because I was always too high.

It wasn't long before I got in trouble with the soccer team. I'd arrived on campus out of shape and a lot heavier than my high school playing weight. I was late for practice regularly, but I always had an excuse. One night during the spring of my freshman year, I binged on ecstasy while hanging out in the dorm. The next morning, I slept through a weight-lifting practice. You just don't do that on an athletic scholarship at a Division I university. You're supposed to act professionally. The coach suspended me from the team.

I would stay suspended until I agreed to go to Twelve Step meetings, stay clean, and go to class. I made sincere and convincing promises to Coach that I'd do better, stay straight, get fit, and fulfill his expectations. The truth is, I really wanted to believe those promises, but I only went to the Twelve Step meetings to get him off my back. I focused more on hiding my using from my teammates while trying to convince Coach that everything was under control. I wasn't playing well or staying in shape.

I could start to see separation within myself. There was that old girl with plans, intentions, and dreams. Then there was the person I was now. It was who I wanted to be and what I wanted to accomplish versus the person and player I was—not adhering to promises, unable to get in shape or make myself a better player. I simply couldn't follow through because I had to keep using.

At the bar and around the dorm smoking pot, I'd tell stories of how good I was growing up—I was a unique player. I told stories of my impending grandeur and success when I made it big. But when alone, I felt guilty. I was hiding out, trapped by isolation and paranoia. I was so fearful of getting caught. I couldn't let my coach, teammates, or parents see me and what I was doing. My double life became more pronounced.

I talked my way back onto the team after the spring season, signing a contract saying I'd stay sober. I sat in Coach's office, looked him in the eye, and wanted so badly to go along with the plan we devised: how to get back in shape, back on track, pull my grades up. But it felt like two little voices were doing battle inside my head. One agreed with him, "I'll turn things around!" But the other one knew I wasn't going to stick to what I had promised. It knew that I was going to walk out of his office and go get high and that I already had plans to go drinking. I tried to suppress that voice to convince Coach and myself, but it was the voice that won.

During my sophomore year, I was still under the contract with my coach not to use, and everyone on the team knew it. During the preseason, the men's and women's soccer teams had a joint initiation party for the freshmen, and I knew everyone there would be drinking. So, rather than let anyone see me drinking at the party, I went to a friend's apartment to have just three shots of vodka and get on a good buzz. I didn't know how to go to a team party sober and didn't want to know how.

MARTHA ■ CONTINUES ON PAGE 59

he was just as accepting as my mother. His first words were, "Are you safe and are you happy?" We had a long embrace, and I felt like I was melting into his safe, loving arms—being reunited with something strong and necessary from my childhood. It was a powerful moment. I am proud of the acceptance I got, especially since too many others are abandoned by their families.

Even while getting reassurance for my sexuality, I remained afraid and, ironically, deeply homophobic. As a gay man, I felt ashamed and thought my masculinity was diminished. I created arbitrary rules about having sex; for example, it could only be an experiment or a few moments of release, always detached from any meaning within a deeper relationship. I began to drink my way through gay bars and clubs so I could follow these "rules," never admitting that I was desperately searching for a way to expel the demons of being abused by my priest and what I still saw as the "demon" of homosexuality.

With college falling away fast as a main concern, I paid the price. I lost my scholarship and left Suffolk altogether without letting my family know. At the next holiday, I told everyone what a great semester I was having, even though I hadn't gone to class in months.

All this time, I was trying to convince family, friends, and myself that I really was making progress in my education and career. In reality, I was running through shorter- and shorter-term jobs as a bartender, parking valet, and waiter—all "careers" designed to facilitate my addictive lifestyle. Switching personas, depending on whom I was around, was just one more tool in playing people to get what I wanted.

FINDING BRAD

The first serious romance of my life was with Brad. He was a few years older than me, and we met at the first gay club I went to. I was drunk but drawn to him; I had to know who he was. When we finally started dating, our entire relationship was influenced by drugs and alcohol. We eventually got drunk and high almost daily.

After three shots, I said, "Oh, I gotta go now and meet the people I'm driving to the party with. See ya later." I walked out of her apartment and then I realized I didn't feel much of a buzz. So I went back up and said, "You know, I've got a while until the party. Why don't I have at least one more drink?" I had a few more and thought I'd feel good enough to have "fun" at the party. I mean I couldn't imagine going out if I wasn't going to drink. I liked myself better drunk and high because I liked how it felt.

My buzz finally started hitting me as I walked into the party. And once I'd started, I was going to need more—my body was asking for more, my mind was demanding more. I started sneaking beer into an opaque glass so no one could see the color of the liquid inside. As hard as I tried to hide all this drinking, by the end of the night, I was the only one dancing—and making a scene because I was the drunkest one there. Drunker than any of the freshmen.

The next day, waking up in the team dorm, I was full of guilt and remorse. How was I gonna get out of this? Everyone on the team saw me drunk. I couldn't believe I'd done it again. But at the same time, I was in survival mode, looking for a way out of trouble. I sat down with my teammates and pleaded with them not to tell Coach. I used every line in the book: "I do have a problem. I want to change, but I can't do it alone. I just need your help, so you can't let Coach know." I had to be as convincing as possible to persuade them not to tell on me. At the same time, it was as if I was trying to convince myself that the game was up, that I had a problem, that I was doing the same things but expecting different results.

I tried to sound sincere, but a voice inside said, "You're not sincere; you're saying every-thing in the moment to get out of this bad situation." I knew that was right and I felt like a fraud. The division within me was causing so much disconnect from who I wanted to be and who I was. I was now an obvious, insincere liar and manipulator. The team didn't tell the coach and I stayed dry more frequently early in the season. I also started to play better. But I knew now that if anyone on the team saw me drunk or high, I was in big trouble. It would be over. Now I really had to cover my tracks. After I smoked pot, I'd spray myself with perfume or chew gum right away. I couldn't go to parties much anymore because I knew I couldn't go sober.

I spent more time with people who weren't on the team so I could use and hide my double life. I found a coke dealer who also had meth. Toward the end of the soccer season, I started using more carelessly. When the season ended, I was relieved because I could do drugs all the time during the off-season. Drugs were my major priority. Part of me still wanted to be an athlete, and part of me didn't anymore. Meanwhile, my actions were those of a drug addict, and the picture I had of myself as an elite athlete became more like an illusion. I was no longer the person I thought I was.

One of my dearest friends came to my room one night. I was high and speedy, but he sat me down and said, "You know, I see this has taken hold of you and you're losing things you love and I'm worried." He looked like he was going to cry. I said, "You're right. I am going

MARTHA ▪ CONTINUES ON PAGE 61

Despite all the drug use, Brad somehow managed to keep a job as a home remodeling designer. I admired how he was always functional and had a nice apartment with furniture and a bed frame, yet could be high most of the time. I didn't get how he did it. I eventually moved in with him, but I kept my old studio apartment, where after more than a year, my mattress was still lying on the floor.

Brad had an electric approach to life, and I saw instantly the fun we could have together. He was comfortable in himself, secure—and a complete partner. That attracted me and I went into our relationship committed to make it work and be monogamous, as I thought normal marriage partners should be. I was trying to make my first serious relationship a perfect one. Of course, that was unrealistic; I was young and needed more experience and knowledge. But being an addict, I lied about that need to Brad and to myself.

Despite the positive feelings, I remained a greedy and calculating person, willing to cheat on him with other men.

Brad seemed loving and committed to me. In my eyes, he was responsible and dedicated to making sure I was okay. At first, I could only bring myself to call Brad my "friend" when introducing him to others, but over time, I felt comfortable and proud calling him my boyfriend. The more I accepted within myself that I was gay, the better I felt about being in a gay relationship.

Despite the positive feelings, I remained a greedy and calculating person, willing to cheat on him with other men. Since this was my first relationship, I felt justified in exploring other possibilities. But rather than honestly telling him what I wanted, I lied—then found more self-righteous rationalizations that vindicated me, at least in my own eyes. Soon I was projecting my own behavior onto Brad, and I became paranoid that he was cheating too. Of course, cheating on Brad threatened his health as well as mine, but I didn't think about that, even though I loved him. That kind of thinking speaks to how strongly addiction had already distorted my behavior and perceptions of reality.

to change, but I hope you don't mind." Then I pulled open a drawer where I'd hidden some lines of coke, and I did the lines right in front of him. That was the power of my addiction.

For spring break, I flew home, but couldn't stop from doing coke in the airplane. I had six drinks before they cut me off. I looked completely whacked out. I couldn't get drunk, and I couldn't come down from the coke. I was a shaky, jumpy, jerky mess with darting eyes and dilated pupils. I got off the plane wearing sunglasses and looking very pale. I'd lost a ton of weight and hadn't showered in days. I had dark circles under my eyes and was sleep deprived from being high on coke.

I knew I couldn't have my family pick me up, so I called some old friends I hadn't seen in a while and they came and got me. I was too jumpy to talk to them coherently, and I wouldn't take off my sunglasses, even inside. It was the worst feeling, trying to pretend I was "normal." They joked with me, "Hey, what's with the glasses? What are you, a movie star?" It took hours before I was down enough to finally go home to my family.

That summer, I got a job in San Diego, so I'd be away from home and able to use. One day, I needed to pick up some more coke, and I found a dealer in San Francisco who had it. So I lied to my friend and borrowed her car for the ten-hour drive. I just had to have the coke, no matter what. In San Francisco, I went on a binge and couldn't drive. My friend had to find someone to drive up with her to retrieve her car—twenty hours total. My behavior was starting to directly damage other people's lives, and all I could say was "Sorry about that."

My world was shrinking and life became more and more closed in. I used to use drugs to make myself more social, but now I used with the shades drawn. I was paranoid, but I couldn't stop. I was so scared; I kept the door locked. I was hearing voices, seeing things in the blinds, and having moments of real darkness. The fun times were few. I'd be up for two to four days and then crash and burn. My hair was a mess and I wore a hat all the time. I was no longer able to look at my eyes in the mirror. My athlete's body was shrinking, losing muscle, and getting really thin.

I decided not to return to Stanford that fall; there was no way I could stop using or could hide it from anyone anymore, so there was no point. I really thought I was hitting bottom. I was scared about what was happening to me. I even thought I was having a heart attack one time while on meth. Finally I went to a forty-five-day treatment program in Arkansas and then entered a halfway house in San Diego. Back on my old turf, I couldn't stay sober. I was in and out of Twelve Step groups, managing thirty days of sobriety, then two weeks, then two months—but always relapsing.

■ MARTHA'S STORY CONTINUES ON PAGE 79 ■

On more than one occasion, Brad rescued me from being late on rent and other bills, even when we weren't living together. I spent my money on K and ecstasy. Without him, I couldn't afford the amount of drugs I was doing. In truth, I cared more about getting high than I did about Brad or anything else. I couldn't even see that addiction was stealing my integrity.

Eventually we loved getting fucked up more than we loved each other. As our relationship stumbled to an end, my addiction became an unstable shield that protected me from feeling anything. I got abusive and blamed Brad, pretending that everything was his problem, not mine. But in the end, I was the one with a serious problem; I was completely addicted to drugs, plowing through my life and other people's lives with a huge ego and low self-esteem.

COPS

Before long, we broke up "for good" and I moved out. About a month later, I was desperate to get high on K. So I called him and we hung out together that evening at a sleazy bar in Cambridge, along with our dealer. We could not get any K or anything else that night, so I got really drunk instead. All night I'd been anticipating getting high. Swallowing my disappointment in drinks, I got more spiteful, angry, and enraged at being denied my drugs.

Soon Brad and I got into a fight. I shoved him, grabbed his car keys, and ran outside. As he chased me, I threw the keys in his face. He turned around, drove off, and left me in Cambridge. I was sloshed and didn't know what to do, so I did what came most naturally to me: went back in the bar for two more shots. Then I persuaded some stranger to drive me back to Boston.

By this time I was in a blackout and the next thing I remember was waking up in jail. However, plenty of people had seen what happened, including the cops, and they made sure I knew eventually.

Apparently I had gone to a former dealer's house to get

some K, but he wasn't home. I kept buzzing his apartment, waking up the neighbors. Then I went back to my old apartment building, banging on the windows and screaming for Brad to come out so I could kill him, despite the fact that Brad had never lived there. In a fit of rage, I broke down the outside door, ran upstairs, and started pounding on the door to my old apartment, where four college students now lived. They called the cops.

Someone else came into the hallway to see what the commotion was, and I threw him against the wall. After I kicked through some windows, the superintendent showed up, and I hit him too. Then the police arrived. As I punched and flailed at them, several cops dragged me outside, where they held my face down on the sidewalk to cuff and arrest me.

I awoke the next morning in a jail cell with nothing more than a little orange juice to handle my huge hangover. No matter how desperately I tried to recall what had happened, I had no memory of how I got there. I was then chained to other prisoners and brought to the Roxbury court holding tank to await my preliminary appearance.

> As usual in a crisis, my first reaction was to push as hard as I could to manipulate the situation to get out of it.

I was scared shitless because I had blacked out. What did I do, kill someone? Do I get a phone call? What's happening to me? As quickly as I could, I tried to snap into my sensible self before stepping in front of the judge. As usual in a crisis, my first reaction was to push as hard as I could to manipulate the situation to get out of it. Any fool, except for an addicted one, would know in two seconds that the experienced judge and cops already had seen every slithering excuse in the book from drunks like me.

When they finally let me use the phone, I called Brad, crying for him to come and rescue me. He took me home to my apartment where we cried together before I crashed for two days. Brad asked, "What were you thinking?" I was stunned when he told me what I'd done.

But I wasn't entirely convinced that Brad and the cops were telling the truth. A few days later, I went back to the apartment building I had attacked and saw a kicked-in door. Then I read the charges against me, including assault and battery on a police officer. I thought, "Shit, I'm gonna get jail time!" The first thing I did was write the cop a letter apologizing. I felt horrible—this is not who I am.

Believe it or not, that moment was my first clue that I might have a problem with drugs.

That thought didn't keep me from doing everything I could to play the system and spin the situation to my advantage. Instead of jail time, I was sentenced to community service. Community service seemed like a noble, if annoying, task, which I quickly got out of by paying a fine. I proceeded to tell other people that I'd only been arrested for disorderly conduct, not assault, and I began to believe it myself. I rationalized my actions by saying, "Every frat guy gets arrested at least once at my age. I may not be in school, but I'm still playing my frat card." Even though our relationship was over, I begged Brad to drive me to my court appearances, where he held my hand while I worked on using this crisis to keep the relationship going.

COMPARATIVE DRUGGING

I had my first hit of ecstasy during my trip to Montreal with Denise when we were both eighteen. We spent all day getting drunk and then spent the evening at a gay bar, where both of us made out with the same man. After that, we went to an after-hours club and came across someone selling E. We figured we couldn't get drunker, so why not try a new drug?

I loved it from the start and told Denise, "Wow, this is a *real* drug." For whatever reason, she didn't feel much and said it was a waste of money, but I was hooked. I lost my jacket, yet I didn't care as I walked sweating and shivering through a park on my way back to the hotel. I sat down for a weird, trippy conversation with a homeless man who spoke no English, while I spoke no French. I had the sensation of flying while still on the ground. So, when we got back to

Boston, I started seeking out gay clubs where I could get E easily.

My Canadian experience made drugs seem cool and fun. Ecstasy gave me a whole new sensation in addition to the buzz I got from drinking. Having that taste of a new high, I soon sought even newer highs.

I still looked down on people who used cocaine because that was something you put up your nose. But this was another of those unrealistic and easy-to-break standards by which addicts live—or should I say by which we slowly kill ourselves?

> I was out of control, trying anything—over and above any limits I had set for myself when I first tried ecstasy.

One night in the basement bathroom of a club, I saw two men using coke in one of the stalls. They thought I was cute and asked me repeatedly to join them. One of the men said, "Hey, just put it in your mouth. It feels like Anbesol!" I thought, "I know what Anbesol is!" and let him put some on my tongue. My mouth did go numb, like he said it would. Making the addict's normal leap of logic, I said to myself, "Anything that makes my mouth numb can't hurt my nose." So, up my nose it went, and I was off.

Over the next few weeks, I was continually hanging out at clubs looking to score small amounts of coke. I'd already befriended and flirted with all the bartenders to get free drinks, so it was easy to use the same method to identify the dealers. One night, at an after-hours club, I got up the courage to score a bag of coke. I wanted to run home and snort it all up right away, even though I was still learning how to handle the stuff, with Al Pacino's role in *Scarface* as my guide.

One night I went looking for ecstasy and pot from one of Brad's ex-dealers, who gave me a line each of special K and crystal meth. I tried them both that night and got completely whacked out. Of course, I wanted more. I was out of control, trying anything—over and above any limits I had set for myself when I first tried ecstasy.

Night of the Living Dead

ROB • DENVER, COLORADO

There was this one night that I am lucky to have lived through. My friends and I had gotten a really early start. By the end of the night, I was on three or four X pills, a couple hits of acid, crystal, and liquor. We were also smoking opium and weed that we had soaked in formaldehyde. I remember that I needed some air because I couldn't breathe in the hot, muggy house, so I went out to the front porch to have a cigarette and chill out in the morning air. I don't know how long I was out there before a friend came out and saw me sitting in the dirt, talking to a little gnome statue in the garden. He said he called my name several times before I snapped suddenly and looked up at him. He said he thought I should try to come down because I didn't look well.

He helped me into the house and laid me on a couch in the back room and then went back to the party. I don't know how long I was lying there or if what happened next was a hallucination or a serious out-of-body experience. Suddenly I was floating and looking down on my very sick body on the couch. This scared the hell out of me and I began ripping at my shirt, trying to pry myself up off the couch. I feared that I was dying and felt that if I could get up and walk around I would be okay. I managed to get out a scream for help, and my friends ran into the room. They were all too messed up to know what to do so they called my roommate, Dave.

Dave came over and immediately took action. He filled the bathtub with cool water, stripped me down, and put me in the tub. He forced me to drink large amounts of water and then stuck his fingers down my throat to induce vomiting. Dave went through this process several times while also pouring cool water over my head in hopes of bringing my temperature down. I can remember my heart beating so fast that I thought it was going to burst through my chest and kill me.

I wasn't coherent enough to even think to pray for God to help me, but I can remember hearing Dave pray as he worked to save my life. After several hours I began to feel better, and Dave drove us home. He laid me in his bed and crawled in next to me. He says he never slept that day, for he feared I would stop breathing at any time.

You would think that would have been enough to make me realize that I was killing myself and ruining my life. NO! Less than two weeks later, I was back at it again. This time I went at it even more hard-core and more often. During that last year of serious partying, I don't know if there was one day I was sober.

I liked meth better than K; I could get more things organized to clean up my messes, the effect lasted longer, and it was cheaper too. Meth let me go for days without eating and seemed to give me the artificial energy to party whenever I wanted. Since I was running away from my life anyway, meth seemed to rescue me.

It was around this time that I met Brad, who was much more into K than I was. Brad had it around often and I decided it was okay. I did all of Brad's K with him. But I hoarded my meth to do alone, when he was at work.

Before doing a drug, I actually researched it—a delusional way of believing that if I knew how a drug affected me I wouldn't OD or do too much. But book knowledge didn't matter and, as alcoholics are fond of saying, "One drink isn't enough, but too many isn't enough, either."

Here's an example of how I saw things: I knew that K, a psychoactive, disassociative downer like PCP, depressed my entire system. But since meth only attacked my nervous system, that meant meth was okay because I knew *exactly* where it attacked—I had researched it! Personal experience soon "backed up" my so-called research. Compared with something like coke, meth kept me awake and feeling high for longer periods. That fact, combined with meth's lower cost, made meth the better bargain in my book. I imagined myself as a well-informed consumer and, as a public service, shared my opinions widely among friends.

Yes, I *really* did think this way.

As I got more involved with Brad, though, I started to do more and more of "his" drug: K. It helped us push the limits of what we did together sexually and lose ourselves in the experience. It turns out we lost ourselves in both senses of the phrase, although I only recognized one sense at the time. K reduced our relationship to getting high, feeling temporarily romantic, and sharing only this narrow experience, rather than sharing any deeper intimacy. I was convinced Brad was a K addict—even though I used it regularly too—and that made him weaker in my mind.

My identity had now become completely entwined with my drugs of choice. As my addiction progressed, it became more and more important to me that I have drinks and drugs that were identified as "mine." That pattern meant putting all my spiritual, emotional, and creative energies into getting high—and nothing else.

METH LIFE

Eventually, my drug became meth. I thought it could make me feel comfortable being alone so I could generate huge amounts of art. I spent countless hours on meth, obsessing about what great things I'd create, and how much I'd do for myself and my friends. Meth felt like it got me thinking more hypersensitively, allowing me to clean out the cobwebs in my mind and giving me strength to accomplish anything in my life. My actual accomplishments while on meth left something to be desired, however.

For example, I'd already been up half the night, very high on meth, when I determined to paint my friend's new apartment for him. He hadn't moved in yet, so, at 4:00 in the morning, I went to a twenty-four-hour Home Depot and bought a power sprayer, which I planned on returning for full credit as soon as I was done using it. "I'll paint everything right now!" I thought. "I'm already up!"

I started spraying the two thousand square feet of walls and stayed up thirty-six straight hours in the process. I had enough meth in me and I was bound and determined to do it all. Here I was obsessing about his apartment when my own place had a half-finished mural on the wall, my mattress and desk lamp still on the floor, and the rent unpaid.

I finally crashed and fell asleep with my face on an ashtray in his sleeping loft. I woke with cigarette butts on my cheeks to the sound of a real estate agent coming through the door to show the apartment to a prospective buyer of the building.

Of course, the paint job was a mess, but I remained proud of my effort. And I never seemed to regain possession of the sprayer so I could return it and get my money back. It became a running joke with my friend; every time I saw him,

I'd ask, "How's my power sprayer doing? Boxed up? Can I come get it?" Over and over we talked about it, but I never retrieved it. For all I know, it's still there.

As I write these stories, I am stunned at how stupidly I acted. I wish I had had a clue of the insanity that my life had become. But this is how I truly lived as an addict—lots of determined talk and promises with virtually no follow-through.

I became very skilled at making a fool of myself.

I'd been up a couple of days on meth when I reported for my shift as a waiter at Milano's Italian restaurant. It was a beautiful day, and many families were out strolling and stopping in for a meal. But I was sweating and frantically running around setting tables, filling Parmesan cheese shakers—doing everything but serving my own tables.

> This is how I truly lived as an addict—lots of determined talk and promises with virtually no follow-through.

Finally, I scrambled over to grace an African American couple with my presence at their table. I tried to put on my professional face, but I was speaking a mile a minute and acting all jittery. When the woman opened her mouth, I thought she would ask for a menu, but instead she said, "Why are you so spastic?" I was furious, but smiled nervously while I thought to myself, "Who does she think she is?" I was embarrassed and humiliated but knew I had to get through this without throwing something at her. My addict's inner crisis voice said, "Get something to eat—quick! That will calm you down."

When I returned to their table, I was still pissed at her, but I forced myself to slow down while reciting the daily specials. I didn't want to blow my cover by giving any more evidence that I was high. Shifting into manipulation at its finest mode, I laid on a sob story that blamed my hyperactivity on how hard I was working and how much homework I had. They asked me what college I went to. After quickly considering, "Hmmm, which one shall I be a student at today?" I said Boston College. I was lucky that Boston is filled with colleges, so I could always dream up one to "attend."

I went on to explain how hard I was studying for exams to make them feel sorry for me and pump up the odds of getting a big tip, even though I'd blown my opening gambit. Of course, it was all a crazed lie—I hadn't been in school for months, and never set foot in Boston College.

But no matter how hard I tried, I couldn't turn off a switch and stop being high. When I brought the salads, I looked down at their crotches to remind myself not to spill anything. I set down the plates and proceeded to ask the man, "Sir, would you like some ground black pecker on your salad?" Only after he stared in shocked amazement at me did I realize what I'd said. I quickly disappeared and demanded that the bartender immediately give me a drink to steady my nerves.

Despite this kind of behavior, the restaurant's manager seemed to like me. I acted very sweet around him and often volunteered to take extra shifts in order to earn more drug money. I was a good salesman and, when on the sober side, a pretty good waiter. I laid it on thick so I could get what I wanted, but more than I deserved, from the job.

But then I started calling in sick because I was too drunk or high to come to work. That meant getting more extreme with my excuses. One time, after spending three days straight at a rave, I called in to say I was recovering from a head injury in a car accident I'd had on my day off. I told the manager, "The doctor says I'll need three days off from work." (That would buy me some time to recover from the rave, do some pot, and sleep.) By now suspicious, he replied, "Okay. But I'll need to see forms from the doctor when you come in."

That was a problem, but not insurmountable. I was in my car with Hillary when I called him, so we just swung around to the neighborhood hospital. At first I thought of just stealing some forms I could fill in myself, but Hillary was afraid we'd get caught and arrested. "Okay," I said, "let's get seen by a doctor, and we can get some pills!" It made sense to me.

So, I saw a doctor, complaining about a concussion and a sore arm. He ordered X-rays and other tests, but I kept him from looking down my throat to see the burn marks from my drug use. I didn't want any professional to see the fresh white skin in my throat that shouldn't be there. After two and a half hours, I had painkillers, official papers to bring to work, and freedom to go out with Denise for drinks. When I went back to Milano's a few days later, I even got sympathy, which made all my efforts worthwhile. I thought I was fooling everyone, but the manager saw through my increasingly lame excuses. He fired me the next time I didn't show up for work. I insisted that I wasn't fired, but rather laid off without pay. It was all their problem, anyway, as far as I was concerned—but I was the one falling apart inside.

BARTENDING 101

Eventually I found bartending jobs at clubs, which gave me a diverse network of party people who seemed to like seeing me. I learned how to sweet-talk my way into after-hours parties and how to get free ecstasy, meth, and special K. That was great because I was in the middle of my breakup and needed something to occupy my time. Plus I could drink while tending bar. Drinking while getting paid for it . . . what could be better?

I got a lot of attention as a bartender, making cocktails shirtless and getting really high. In fact, I can remember getting so fucked up on K that I couldn't even count my money at the end of the shift. Still, I felt like I was getting away with murder, all while being barely present to the reality in which I was living.

The people I hung around almost justified my insane lifestyle of partying, staying physically fit, and traveling to circuit parties. They made me think my life had a purpose. Meanwhile, my art had disappeared. I was consumed by drugs, getting high, and having sex. My purpose in life was to look good on the outside and scramble to pay my rent and get my drugs for the week.

More and more, I felt desperate and hopeless, absolutely at the end of my rope. By then, around the time of my arrest, I was thinking about getting help—but wasn't ready to ask for it.

Side Effects

WHAT YOU NEED TO KNOW

Sex and Drugs

Alcohol and drug use almost always lead to dangerous sexual behavior—unless, of course, you drink so much that you pass out or use certain drugs that depress your sex drive, resulting in no sex at all. Your ability to make good decisions disappears when you are under the influence, as does your ability to remember the negative consequences of your actions. Not using a condom, having sex with someone on the "sketchy" side or even a stranger, or being the victim of date rape—any of these behaviors could result in pregnancy, sexually transmitted diseases like herpes, chlamydia, gonorrhea, and syphilis, or one of the most serious side effects of all: contracting HIV/AIDS.

Other side effects of having sex while using are less concrete but still damaging. You might sleep around so much that you destroy your reputation, especially if you're still in high school. You might sexually abuse someone else. While your victim suffers physical effects, you will have psychological repercussions that are difficult to treat.

Finally, if you use, have sex, and become pregnant, you risk giving birth to a baby who has to go through withdrawal or has birth defects. Think ahead to a future in which you might want to have children. Know that studies have shown that using drugs can cause infertility in women and lower sperm counts in men.

Acne

Although no scientific evidence links substance abuse to acne, users do report breakouts and eruptions in the skin. Drugs such as crystal methamphetamine, for example, have been known to cause mild to severe acne, which users refer to as "speed bumps." Poor diet and hygiene may contribute to the condition, which understandably wreaks havoc on the self-esteem of adolescents and young adults in recovery.

Your skin health is often an indication of your overall health; breakouts related to drug use should subside as your recovery progresses. Regular cleansing (see www.acne.org for a reliable daily regimen) and a healthy diet will keep skin in good condition as you get on with your clean life.

Meanwhile, if you do have acne, clean your skin daily with a mild soap or nonfragrant cleanser, being careful not to irritate your skin. Mild antibacterial cleansers are also available.

Avoid buffing the skin with an abrasive or brush, as scrubbing too hard can actually make acne worse. Do not pick at or squeeze pimples, as this can cause scarring and infection. Use an over-the-counter benzoyl peroxide product on problem areas; benzoyl peroxide can cause redness and drying, so look for creams or lotions with a lower concentration of the active ingredient, say 2.5 percent, to start. A moisturizer specially designed for acne treatment may also be used to counteract dryness. If you suffer severe acne, your doctor or dermatologist may prescribe an oral tablet or a topical antibiotic that can be applied to your skin. To cover blemishes, use a nongreasy product formulated to match skin color and available at the drugstore.

Note: Alcoholics who are taking Antabuse, a drug that makes them ill if they swallow even the least bit of alcohol, should not use creams, lotions, ointments, or other skin products containing alcohol. The alcohol can be absorbed through the skin and could make a patient on Antabuse sick.

Smoking

Cigarette smoking and substance abuse go hand in hand. Between 80 and 95 percent of alcoholics and substance abusers smoke. And tobacco is a known gateway drug; for teens especially, smoking often leads to substance abuse. Many substance abusers also use tobacco in recovery, the one dependence they think they can hang on to as they try to give up alcohol or other drugs. But more and more rehab centers and addiction specialists feel that giving up smoking is a critical part of recovery; in fact, some experts say your treatment depends on it. Studies have found that cigarette smokers relapse to their primary drugs of choice more often, more frequently, and sooner than nonsmokers do. In one study, people who continued to use nicotine had a recovery rate of 12 percent while those who did not had a 59 percent recovery rate. All the more reason to quit smoking at the same time you deal with your alcohol or other drug dependency.

Nicotine is highly addictive in a way that is similar to cocaine or heroin. Smoking a cigarette distributes nicotine to your brain very quickly, stimulating your central nervous system and producing an almost immediate nicotine high. Beginning smokers may experience headaches and coughing, but in general smokers feel less tense and better able to concentrate after only a few puffs on a cigarette. These effects soon go away, but the attraction is so great, smokers usually want to repeat the experience.

Once you develop a tolerance for nicotine, you need to smoke more to achieve the desired results. Tolerance leads to greater dependency and addiction, and most smokers continue to smoke not only to feel the pleasurable effects of smoking, but also to avoid the negative effects of withdrawal. The symptoms of withdrawal from nicotine, which can be felt within a few hours of a last cigarette, may include cravings, irritability, hunger, sleep disturbance, confusion, an inability to focus, aggression, and anger.

Cigarette smoking is the leading preventable cause of death in the United States. How best to quit differs from one smoker to the next, but self-help

4

A Turning Point

THE AWAKENING

If you see a drunken homeless person on the street or a writhing teenager in an emergency psych ward, you might think, "Oh, they've hit bottom." But you'd be wrong. Bottoming out is internal, not external. You can't observe it; you can only feel it. »

In the language of recovery from addiction, there are many metaphors for our need to stop using. We talk about hitting bottom, breaking through the wall of denial, and "getting sick and tired of being sick and tired." Most of these sound dreadful—but the life of an addict is dreadful.

SOULS OF MUD

I had a bed, but I never put together the bedposts. I figured people would think the mattress on the floor looked Zen, but it was actually sad. I started, but never finished, a mural of a rose and tribal figure dancing around the barren walls in the bedroom. I never opened the curtains. I never put away the papers, unopened bills, dusty CD covers, unfolded laundry, and dirty plates scattered across the floor. The smallest chores became the biggest tasks, and I didn't do them. My room was just a messy storage facility I used for coming down after parties and getting ready to go to more.

I left drugs out around the apartment and cut straws in the kitchen. I steamed K on a shiny porcelain plate in the microwave to crystallize it, and then I'd cut the residue into a powder and use it. Several times, I just left the plate in the microwave and scattered other paraphernalia carelessly around the place. I stayed isolated from my roommates like a fearful child, just paying the rent and leaving. I was in a depressed, disgusting, and lonely state.

Still deluded that I was progressing as an artist, I had erratic moments of painting furiously. One time, I got high on meth and stayed up two straight days painting while no one else was home. In my mind, I'd create a stunning master-piece, with people dancing, unique textures, and vivid colors. The painting was so successful that I could see souls dancing through the canvas.

I explained all this to my roommate John and his girlfriend when they came home on the second day. They looked at me strangely but didn't say anything. When I came down off my trip, I saw why—nothing was on the canvas but streaks of muddy, filthy paint. I realized that their silent stares were looks of disgust. I thought I was Picasso, but I was only hallu-cinating, making a fool of myself. This was one of the first times I felt completely humiliated by drugs.

I thought I was Picasso, but I was only hallucinating, making a fool of myself.

I was also starting to have paranoid hallucinations. When someone ran into my car and drove away, I was convinced people were out to get me. A few days before, I'd received junk mail from some group, which I took as evidence that a cult was trying to take over my mind and wreck my car. I called my mother repeatedly to explain how I was in danger and ask for her help. But the only danger was from inside me.

Many old friends started walking away from me, and I walked away from them because they weren't partying like I was. They didn't want to be around the person I was when I got fucked up. I didn't want to see how and why they were leaving, so I didn't. Instead, I surrounded myself with nightlife party people and dealers.

How could I not see what was happening around me and the bizarre distortions going on in my thinking? Because, as I said early on, denial is the most stubborn symptom of addic-tion. Fortunately for me, while things continued downhill,

I started to see a few small cracks of light in the thick wall of my own denial.

Bridget and I worked together at one of the many restaurants where I was employed. I enjoyed hanging out with her even after I got fired. We'd sometimes be at the same parties, although she'd make herself scarce if I started doing a lot of drugs. We sometimes had espresso martinis together at Sunday brunches in a neighborhood restaurant. I thought we had a great relationship. One day we were on the phone trying to make a date for lunch when Bridget said, "Chris, don't bother, because I cannot rely on you."

I was stunned. I'd always thought of myself as honest and dependable. Even after addiction had overwhelmed my life, I'd convinced myself that I still had morals and integrity. Now, a friend was saying I couldn't be counted on anymore.

In that moment, I had a glimpse of clarity and I could sense what was wrong. The glimpse didn't last. But the deeply imprinted memory of Bridget's words did. From then on, whenever I got fucked up on drugs, I'd hear her saying, "Don't bother; I can't trust you." This small awakening wasn't enough to break my addictions. However, in my mind, Bridget's words became attached to some emotional need to find a solution to my fucked-up life. Some part of me knew that I craved guidance and help.

That guidance dropped into my life just about then, although it would be almost a year before I took firm hold of it.

ANDREW

I met my next boyfriend, Andrew, in the same restaurant where I met Bridget. Andrew was older, engaging, more open than most people I knew, and he seemed genuinely interested in me. He had handsome brown eyes, Italian skin tone, and salt-and-pepper hair. Andrew's heart always seemed connected to his smile, and he exuded the kind of character that could fill a room.

For my addiction, a relationship with Andrew was good timing. I wasn't ready to give up using, and he enjoyed a good party and having fun. He drank a lot, but not as much as I did. Still, despite my growing drug intake, he saw me as someone he could support, mentor, befriend, and love. When we first dated, he sent me orchids that hadn't yet bloomed. They seemed symbolic of the renewal and new growth I wanted in my life before I met him—a renewal I wasn't yet sick enough to seek.

Andrew's love felt unconditional to me. I used his love and support as a crutch and shield to go out and screw myself up big time on drugs and alcohol. During our first few months together, I lied about my drug dealing, how much alcohol and other drugs I was using, and the danger I was putting myself in—as I had with so many others in the past.

Still, Andrew saw potential in me. He encouraged my art by getting me supplies and letting me paint at his place. He said he saw brilliance in me that was clouded and caught in a web of fear and addiction. I can see now that Andrew provided me the strength to start pushing through the fears that kept me high, so I could figure out what I was doing to myself. His faith and trust in me, even during my darkest days, helped propel me into a place of healing. He believed in me enough that I was eventually able to start believing in myself.

I used his love and support as a crutch and shield to go out and screw myself up big time on drugs and alcohol.

Even though I loved Andrew, I wanted him to abandon and discard me because everything in my life had become so self-destructive by then. I was stunned when he didn't bail out. Instead he offered me open arms like the sculpture that Sister Vera loved so much. While our romantic relationship couldn't survive my last days of using, Andrew still somehow continued to stand by me as a friend as I finally began my recovery.

I continued to get fired from restaurants and bars. On Gay Pride Day—also my birthday—I was supposed to work an evening shift starting at 5:00 at Blackstone's in the South End. The big parade was during the day, so I went to watch

Elite Player, Extreme User

MARTHA • FORT WORTH, TEXAS

▪ MARTHA'S STORY CONTINUES FROM PAGE 61 ▪

No longer were drugs interfering with school, family, soccer, friendships, or relationships. Life now was interfering with my drugging.

An old friend confronted me about my using during this time. As I held a bottle of vodka and a bag of coke in the air, I asked, in all seriousness, "Do you really think I have a problem and need help?" She just peered at me and said, "Looking at you is like looking through a pair of bifocals; everything about you is blurry. We're watching you disappear before our eyes. You're disintegrating from the inside out."

I understood what she said. Even today, I haven't found better words to describe how I felt. My spirit and soul were decaying from their core. I was empty and the emptiness was starting to come from within and grow outward. She could see in my eyes that nothing was behind them. I was detaching from my self and spirit.

I was now breaking all promises, large and small, to family and friends. When they called, I avoided making any commitments to get together. Later in the week, I'd have to cancel even these vague plans or any other appointments. My internal "cutoff time" for drugging and drinking got later and later in the day. I had crossed another line. I couldn't even uphold the image of living a double life or hiding my drug use. Now when someone called, it was just, "Look, I can't show up. I'm in no condition." And I didn't even apologize.

The following year, Stanford had a new soccer coach. I made an agreement with him that I could come back if I stayed clean for one year and got in shape. Two weeks before I was supposed to return, I started smoking crack. As a result, I was asked to leave my grandmom's house. I moved in with a sober friend, but I'd lost another opportunity, another part of my dreams. I had to call the coach and say I couldn't return because I hadn't stayed sober.

My sober roommate gave me an ultimatum: if I kept using, I'd have to leave. I had no place else to go. My parents weren't speaking to me and didn't want me near them. My connection with my family was nothing but pain, distance, and heartache. I managed to get a job and stayed sober for five months. But one day at work, the urge to smoke dope started calling to me.

My roommate planned to pick me up from work so I could go home and get through the rest of the day sober. But the drugs called to me too strongly. I called her from work and said not to pick me up. She knew I was going to go get high, and she started crying into the phone. She knew I was saying that drugs were more important than everything else. I was even willing to risk having no place to live, just to get high.

I left work and took a cab to a motel room, where I spent the night drinking and shooting coke and crack with a dealer and addict. I remember having brief moments when I looked around the motel room and I didn't recognize myself anymore. Here I was in a Fort Worth motel I'd passed by since I was a kid. From the outside, it was old, familiar territory.

MARTHA ▪ CONTINUES ON PAGE 81

and told myself, "You have to work tonight, so don't drink this afternoon." But as soon as I got to the parade, I started doing K. By 3:00, I was a mess. Andrew and some of his friends were also at the parade; they were drinking and feeling care-free, while my friends and I were obsessively drugging.

Showing no respect for the restaurant's owners, I showed up for work on time, drunk, and high. My birthday present was getting fired on the spot. It turns out that this really was a gift, because it was a consequence directly related to my addiction. I didn't want to get fired anymore. I didn't want to lie or hurt anymore, either.

But within a few days, I had another job tending bar. I always succeeded in lining up my next job, so I was able to maintain my cycle of charming people for tips and teasing patrons for drugs. I sold some drugs on the side to keep money coming in too. But I couldn't keep myself together after the workday was done. Paranoia and craziness had infiltrated my life.

Andrew recently told me a story that I didn't remember, but I'm sure it happened, given the shape I was in.

> We were sitting on the couch in my apartment. You were upset and crying about something and started talking about what had happened with the priest when you were young. I wanted to let you keep talking about it because I thought that would help reduce the shame and help you recognize that his abuse wasn't your fault.
>
> But then you turned to me with tears in your eyes, and I heard this little boy's voice come out of your grown man's body and say, "He'll come over here and break my legs."
>
> Even though you were an adult, you were still absolutely terrified that Father would find you and hurt you all those years later, just because you told someone what had happened.
>
> You were dead serious and truly believed this. It scared me to see how scared you were by this old threat, which had no chance of ever being carried out. It was then that I realized how much you had lost touch with reality, and that you needed far more help than I could give you.

But inside that motel room, I couldn't believe where my life had taken me. I had no school, no scholarship, no family, no money, and no place to live. Now I was sharing IV needles, and I had no idea how it was ever going to stop. I wanted to get high so much that my addiction was choking me and possessing me. I was scared that night. I remember knowing I was scared and into something I truly had no power over. And I didn't know what to do.

The next day, my family and a few friends did yet another intervention with me. A woman I grew up with was there, and she got tears in her eyes when she saw my bruised arms. She said, "Why do you do this to yourself?" For the first time in my life, I didn't have an answer or excuse. I truly didn't know what was going on or why I was doing these things.

That left me so scared of the disease's power that I was willing to go to a hospital. While I was detoxing, I paced the floor. I felt like I couldn't take the anxiety anymore, so I called my dealer and said, "Come get me." Then I told him to wait until I called him back. I couldn't decide what I really wanted to do. I looked out the window. It was cloudy, cold, and gross out. I thought, "If he comes and gets me, where will I go from here? I know I can't stop anymore." I knew this moment was like jumping off a cliff into the unknown. I was deciding whether I lived or died, whether I began roaming the streets, living with this dealer, or stealing money to buy drugs. Still, a strong part of me wanted to get high. I wanted that rush from shooting coke so badly. But I didn't call the dealer back.

That night, a couple of people from a Twelve Step program came to the hospital and told their stories. For once, I could hear what they were saying. One woman's coke addiction had taken her to similar places that mine had. She said she finally understood the reality that no amount of coke would ever be enough. When she asked me, "Would you ever have enough?" I knew the answer was no. I knew I'd do all the coke I could, or it would kill me, or I'd be paralyzed by the fear of running out. A room stuffed full of cocaine wasn't enough for me.

My first spiritual experience, my turning point, was to hear those people that night.

A few days later, some friends and my mother came with a backpack for me and asked me if I was willing to go to long-term treatment in New Jersey. I said yes, figuring it would be three to five months. It turned out to be ten and a half months in a facility with no phone calls, no gym, not even magazines. But that's what I needed. I needed physical separation. Couldn't do it any other way. It changed my life.

■ MARTHA'S STORY CONTINUES ON PAGE 98 ■

Andrew wasted no time in suggesting that I get therapy to understand the deep feelings of pain that caused me to act out and continue my destructive pattern. "I care too much about you to watch you fall apart," he said. "I'll help you. I'm willing to do anything at all to help you be okay. But you clearly need professional help." Soon he'd hooked me up with Jerry, an amazing therapist who specialized in adult male survivors of child sexual abuse.

GETTING THE TREATMENT

Jerry began every therapy session by asking me what my drug and alcohol intake had been the previous week. I lied, of course, and told him it was less than what I actually took. That didn't stop him from recognizing my addiction.

I was insulted. I thought, "I'm paying for this! He should be grateful I'm here making him money. I don't need to pay someone to tell me to get help with drugs. I'm getting help here!" Jerry was insistent that my most immediate problem was addiction, but he also knew that he couldn't push me too hard at first or else I would bolt.

During every session, Jerry said I should think about going to a Twelve Step group, and he told me about nearby young people's meetings. To get him to stop nagging me, I said I'd start going to a few Twelve Step meetings. Because I went only to get Jerry off my back, I didn't get much out of them. My drinking, drugging, and paranoia just got worse until finally Jerry said I needed treatment for my addiction.

Andrew backed up that decision, and so I entered a thirty-day outpatient rehab at Fenway Community Health Center in the fall. In addition to Twelve Step principles, Fenway used acupuncture and meditation as part of the program. I thought it was a riot seeing people with needles stuck in them; they looked like they were in a *Saturday Night Live* skit. But once I tried it, the acupuncture seemed to help me too. So did counselors like Rosemary, with her calm and loving voice that reminded me of my mother. I felt safe and loved.

When treatment was over, I felt better and managed to stop using drugs. I didn't stop drinking, though, and my alcohol intake tripled to make up for the absence of drugs. Still, it felt like the part of my mind that had gone dormant was finally working again. True, I woke up every day with a hangover, but at least my bed wasn't on the floor anymore, with a vial nearby to do lines first thing in the morning. But because I was now drinking like a fish, Jerry strongly suggested getting Twelve Step help with my alcohol use. I responded by lying to him about how much I was drinking.

After treatment, I felt like I'd made a completely new start. I went out and got a brand-new job—tending bar. If getting a job tending bar straight out of drug treatment sounds laughable, it is. But it is also an example of how our denial can be so stubborn that we addicts can truly believe that bars are fine places to get over drug addiction. I also believed that since Andrew was still drinking, it was no problem for me to keep drinking too.

SAINT MARTIN INTERVENES

That January, Andrew and I decided to take a short vacation to the French side of Saint Martin in the Caribbean. I thought this was a great idea and a prize I'd earned for just getting off drugs. I thought, "I'll reward myself for being clean and sober by relaxing on the beach with cocktails and beer. It'll be a good experience and a great way to get away from the New England cold!"

Saint Martin is a beautiful island, and walking barefoot on the sand was a great sensation. So was having frozen drinks brought to us on the beach. There was a lovely beer I'd never tasted before called Carib—just like Corona. It was even better than Corona, though, because it was only one dollar, with a lime included!

One day, we heard about an after-dark, full-moon beach party that night on the Dutch side of the island. I'd been drinking while we collected seashells throughout the afternoon, and I had martinis and wine at dinner. Even though he

Praying for Water

DAVID • SEATTLE, WASHINGTON

It was a guy at a party who "helped" me hit bottom. He was already fully loaded and anxious for me to catch up. He fed me enough tina to last me a few nights, but all in the course of an hour's time. I kept telling him I was fine, to let me slow down. He kept urging me and pushing me to catch up to him. Then I realized that something was drastically wrong.

Beads of sweat began rolling down the sides of my face. My eyes were rolling around in my head, and I was having trouble focusing. I remember begging this creep to let me take a shower to cool off and calm down, all the while he was cursing at me for ruining his night. When he tossed me out of the house, I immediately fled to my car and hid (I was paranoid a cop might find me and arrest me). My heart was beating faster and faster, and I kept checking my neck pulse, which was beating out of control. In my car, I fixated on the almost-full moon. I was sure at this point I was going to die. So I looked at the moonlight and began speaking to God. It may have been anywhere from two to four hours, but I prayed for God to spare my life.

By now, my tongue was so parched I began to feel as if I could swallow it. I HAD to get water. I didn't know the neighborhood I was in, and there was no way that I would drive. I was so disoriented, but I fixated on the need for water. I got out of my car and began looking for a deli or 7-Eleven. Along the way, I put my mouth on people's dirty garden hoses and guzzled water like a homeless thief in the middle of the night. I was a wreck. Finally a nice man pointed me in the direction of a nearby deli where I got several bottles of water and somehow wandered back to my car. I now believe that God sent this man to help me.

I guess another hour went by. My eyes remained on the moon as I drank water and prayed until well after sunup. My heart rate didn't slow down for hours, but I kept focused, prayed, and bargained, and somehow I made it through. I took three days off from work and sweated the garbage out of my system, drinking gallons of water to flush it out of me. I couldn't sleep, but at this point I was scared to death of taking even a sleeping pill. I just gritted my teeth and clenched my jaws for hours on end. Every time I walked past a mirror, I would look at myself, see dark circles under baggy eyes and rosy, acne-like rashes on my cheeks, and cry. What had I done to myself?

And this, my friends, is the day I decided never to pick up another drug (tina or any other) again. No program, no treatment, I just quit! I do believe with all of my heart and soul that God spared me that night. I do believe that he wanted me to do more with my time and the love that I have to give others.

had much less to drink, Andrew was tired after we ate, so I brought him back to the hotel where he went to sleep.

Then I went off to find directions to the beach party. I planned to sober up a bit, and then drink a lot when I got there. I didn't know the island well, but I drove Andrew's rental car, a little Kia, to the other side of the island anyway. After all, I always drove drunk in Boston and never had any trouble.

The steel drums played and smoke from the beach bonfire mixed with smoke from the pot—but I wasn't smoking any. I was superior because I'd said no to drugs, and so I felt great getting more and more drunk. Since it was after 1:00 in the morning, I made sure I had ice in all of my drinks. I had a long-held theory that ice would provide enough hydration to allow me to drive safely home if I was still drinking after 1:00.

> I was superior because I'd said no to drugs, and so I felt great getting more and more drunk.

Around 3:00, I decided to drive back to the French side and our hotel. I felt really trashed, but there was no way I was going to hitch a ride. I got in the car, and right away I felt like the Kia was driving me back while I watched from the sidelines.

It was raining and everything looked blurry, so I focused on the music coming from the car radio instead of the road. Saint Martin is a small island with lots of hills, so the roads have many hairpin turns with concrete guardrails and lane dividers. I was going so fast around them that I felt like I was driving the Monaco Grand Prix.

In a drunken stupor, swerving hard to avoid one of the dividers, I didn't realize that the Kia might spin out. It did. Then it hit the side of a small bridge over a creek and went flying through the air. My life flashed before my eyes and I remember vividly seeing my family and my death. Then the Kia landed on its side in a ditch.

The next thing I remember was worrying whether the shells we collected were okay in the back seat, because if they were broken, I'd have a hard time explaining what had happened to Andrew. I hung upside down in the seat belt, looking at the cracked windshield, feeling my face for blood and wondering if I were dead. Then I had a flashing moment of gratitude for surviving the crash, followed by terror over being in deep shit in a foreign country, where I might be arrested for DUI and thrown into a dirty cell with nothing to eat or drink but bad water. I needed to get the fuck out of the car and away from the scene as soon as I could.

The Kia's engine was still running and its wheels spinning. Remembering old episodes of *MacGyver,* I thought the car would explode in a ball of fire. So my adrenaline kicked in, I rescued the seashells, and I got the hell out.

I had a flashing moment of gratitude for surviving the crash, followed by terror over being in deep shit in a foreign country.

Behind the wreck, a line of cars backed up on the narrow road. A large Caribbean man came over and stopped me from running while he ran his big black hands over my face to see if I was okay. I had the sensation that he was like God for me just then, but at the same time I wanted him to get his hands off of me so I could run.

In one of the cars was a group of French kids I'd seen at the beach party. I ran up to them and said, in broken French, "You have to get me out of here!" They took me to their hotel, in the middle of nowhere, where I passed out for a while. I finally convinced them to drive me back to my hotel.

I felt numb, raw, and scared. I'd destroyed Andrew's rental car and fled the scene of an accident in a foreign country. How would I lie to get out of this one? Suddenly I came up with what seemed like a foolproof story: I'd been carjacked and the thieves had wrecked the car! I desperately wanted to avoid the consequences of what had happened, even if it was just for the moment. More than anything, I needed to sleep.

I woke Andrew up and said that a tragedy had happened. I'd been carjacked—but I had the seashells! I told him not to worry and that we'd talk in the morning. I fell into bed, but in the morning the truth began to come out. The first major hole in my carjacking story was the discovery that I still had the Kia's keys in my pocket. I've kept them ever since as a reminder of that night.

I somehow persuaded Andrew to report the car to the police as stolen. But I immediately resented having to go along to the police station because it was hot out. My clothes clung to my body as I sweated alcohol. My mouth was dry and the glaring sun hurt my eyes. I was hung over, and I wanted to get on to drinking lunch when we were done. I thought my biggest problem was having forgotten my sunglasses that morning. This was the closest I'd ever come to dying, but within hours I acted like it was no more serious than getting caught pulling the fire alarm at school.

And by the time we got back to Boston, our romance was finished.

AROUND ANOTHER CURVE

No matter how lightly I treated the accident in Saint Martin, it began to weigh heavily on my mind when I got home. I knew I'd been granted the miracle of having a stark life-and-death incident directly related to my alcohol use. I also knew I wanted to choose life over death. I went back to Jerry and told him, "I can't risk my life like this anymore or hurt those around me. I've destroyed Andrew's trust in me. If I get behind the wheel again, the alcoholic

A Teenager's Tears of Hope

JANE • ONTARIO, CANADA

JANE'S STORY CONTINUES FROM PAGE 19

I'm fifteen, and every time I went for a drink I was waiting to die. I tried every strategy: getting into cars with drunk drivers, going home with anybody, and eventually trying to commit suicide three times by taking pills, hanging, and cutting myself. No luck. Finally, my mom put me in a treatment center. I came in unwillingly, expecting a bunch of retards who couldn't control their drinking, bums, hookers, crackheads, losers. That wasn't me. I thought I was the complete opposite—cool, clean-cut, with class and style. Wrong. These people were my age, struggling to fight the disease called alcoholism. They looked normal and didn't seem to smell or act funny. So I checked in, planning to party harder when I got out.

I started to have withdrawal shakes, sweating, moodiness, and, worst of all, I was probably the most insane person in there. Then the weirdest thing happened. I began to follow the program in treatment, and I went to some AA meetings. I finally cried, not out of anger, guilt, or shame, but with tears of hope that I could survive, not for anybody or anything else, but for me. I graduate this Saturday. I'm very scared.

will take over and kill me, or someone else. This is it—I now know I have a problem with drinking as well as with the other drugs."

But after I left Jerry's office, I still wasn't connecting all the dots. I knew I could no longer exist drinking like an alcoholic, but I continued to think I could control my drinking. I decided that I wouldn't get drunk anymore, but I wasn't yet prepared to entirely get rid of alcohol in my life.

I tried to dry myself out and occasionally went to Twelve Step meetings, but I also kept tending bar. I didn't do any drugs, so I thought I was "sober." At meetings, I tried to pay attention and be present, but I was scared shitless. I thought, "These people are crazy, not like me. I'm special. They need this program. I don't." I thought I was doing them a favor by gracing them with my presence. I put myself above every alcoholic and addict I saw there.

Even though I knew intellectually that I was an alcoholic and that alcoholics can never drink safely, I somehow believed I was different.

So I kept on drinking and getting drunk. Even though I knew intellectually that I was an alcoholic and that alcoholics can never drink safely, I somehow believed I was different. And I acted accordingly. This is what Twelve Steppers call "engaging in terminal uniqueness."

Eventually I needed a drink to prepare myself for a meeting. I'd drink a 36-ounce vodka with cranberry juice and then walk in the door. I would sit and twitch, shake, and sweat. I tried to listen and understand, but mostly I stared at the clock waiting for the meeting to end so I could bolt. And I did this over and over again. Finally I realized that I wasn't different. Even though I was younger than most (but not all) of the others in the room, I was just like them.

So I stopped drinking. I went to the gym every day and worked out. I felt great. On my third day without a drink, a beautiful snow fell and I felt like I was walking peacefully through a snow globe on my way to the gym. This was a truly wonderful way to live, and so I decided to celebrate it.

If you're an alcoholic or addict, you know what's coming next. I called up my friend Reed, because we liked to drink together. We met at an Irish pub, where I sat at the bar and had a martini. And another. And then some more. I knew from the first sip that I was on pattern to get smashed. Reed was an accomplice, but I didn't really need him for what I was doing. We talked awhile and then went bar hopping, making sure to stop at places where I knew the bartenders and could get a free drink. Late that night when last call came at the last bar, I ordered four drinks and downed them all before sending Reed home in a cab.

I stumbled home, followed by a guy who was cruising me. I didn't know him, but I let him follow me. I took him up to my room because I knew he'd have sex with me. I went to the bathroom, and when I came back to my room, he was standing there naked, staring at me, and begging me to urinate on him.

Even though I was completely wasted, I knew I'd put myself in a crazy, disgusting, and potentially dangerous situation. Thinking that this guy was a nut, I forced him to put his clothes back on. Violently enraged, I pushed him down three flights of stairs and threw him out of the house. The whole time, I was thinking, "Look what this guy has done to me!"

By the next day, it was finally clear to me that it wasn't this guy, or anyone else in my past, who had done this to me. My addiction and I had done this to me.

That was February 4, 2001—the day I finally gave in to the fact that I am an alcoholic/addict, and the day I began to surrender to all that fact means in my life. I started by going to a Twelve Step meeting that night; ironically it was on "K" Street in the Fenway.

As of today, I haven't had a drink or drug since. However, getting from there to here was hard, and sometimes not a pretty story.

Finding Help

Twelve Step Programs

Everyone has heard of AA or Alcoholics Anonymous. But did you know there are Narcotics Anonymous (NA), Marijuana Anonymous (MA), Crystal Meth Anonymous (CMA), Cocaine Anonymous (CA), and more? As the number of chemical substances we use has increased, so, too, has the number of Twelve Step programs. They all share the same basic philosophy, based on the famous Twelve Steps:

1. We admitted we were powerless over alcohol—that our lives had become unmanageable.

2. Came to believe that a Power greater than ourselves could restore us to sanity.

3. Made a decision to turn our will and our lives over to the care of God *as we understood Him*.

4. Made a searching and fearless moral inventory of ourselves.

5. Admitted to God, to ourselves, and to another human being the exact nature of our wrongs.

6. Were entirely ready to have God remove all these defects of character.

7. Humbly asked Him to remove our shortcomings.

8. Made a list of all persons we had harmed, and became willing to make amends to them all.

9. Made direct amends to such people wherever possible, except when to do so would injure them or others.

10. Continued to take personal inventory and when we were wrong promptly admitted it.

11. Sought through prayer and meditation to improve our conscious contact with God *as we understood Him,* praying only for knowledge of His will for us and the power to carry that out.

12. Having had a spiritual awakening as the result of these steps, we tried to carry this message to alcoholics, and to practice these principles in all our affairs.

Recovery through a Twelve Step program involves going to meetings, finding a sponsor, "working" the Steps, reading program literature, and eventually holding service positions. Twelve Step programs are spiritual but not religious; there is no specific religious affiliation, and if you don't believe in a traditional God, you are free to substitute

90

whatever concept you want to use as your Higher Power. Members have thought of love, nature, even the group itself as their Higher Power. Twelve Step programs are not a cult; there is no financial obligation and no membership requirements other than the desire to stop drinking or using. Members are told to "take what they like and leave the rest."

Meetings are held regularly throughout the country and all over the world, often in churches, hospitals, or other community locations. In large cities like New York, you can find meetings every day of the week. Smaller towns might only have one or two meetings a week. Look in the yellow pages of a phone book for a telephone number to call for meeting times and places.

The type of Twelve Step program you choose depends on a couple of factors. If your drug of choice is alcohol, you'd go to AA. If it's pot, cocaine, crystal, or some other substance, you usually can go to AA as well as NA, MA, and so forth. Certain meetings may be more open to accepting members whose primary addiction is not the main focus of that group. The flavor of meetings varies a lot, so if there are more than one or two meetings where you live, you're encouraged to check them all out before deciding if the program is for you or not. More and more, especially in major cities, there are meetings with a focus on a specific group: teens and young adults, gays and lesbians, Spanish speakers.

Twelve Step programs for the family and friends of alcoholics and addicts are called Al-Anon, Nar-Anon, Alateen, and so forth. Based on the same Twelve Steps, these programs evolved when it was discovered that chemical dependency is a disease that affects everyone it comes into contact with. If you decide to join a Twelve Step program, you might want to suggest Al-Anon to your loved ones. (See pages 115 and 137.)

Types of Treatment

Most people who need addiction treatment—depending on insurance coverage—need to decide whether to enter a residential facility or attend an outpatient treatment program. Both residential and outpatient treatment are effective in addressing addiction and alcoholism.

Residential Treatment

Residential treatment, sometimes called "inpatient treatment," provides more of the necessary services for the multiple problems facing a recovering addict. Residential treatment also seems to be better for people who have extreme addictions, certain medical and psychiatric problems, and little social support. People with less severe problems do just as well in outpatient care.

Residential treatment offers certain advantages, which include

• providing complete immersion into recovery

• safeguarding patients from the addictive substances

• immediately limiting further damage to the family

• providing more time for therapy and peer interaction

Outpatient Treatment

The majority of people in addiction treatment are in outpatient programs. These programs are more available, less expensive, and less disruptive to school or work.

Outpatient treatment is usually offered two to three hours a day, several times per week. The programs are set up with day and evening hours, and at first, the services are more intense and frequent, perhaps for the first month, and then diminish over time. Treatment lasts for six to twelve weeks, but it can last for up to a year or more. The treatment itself is based on the same principles as residential treatment, and it is as effective as residential treatment for those with less severe illness. Outpatient treatment, however, lacks the extensive variety of services and multidisciplinary team members available in residential care.

Outpatient programs have a higher dropout rate, and participants are more prone to alcohol and other drug use during the treatment experience. Participants attend treatment while remaining in the environment in which they were using alcohol and other drugs, which can be very difficult without proper support. Weigh these factors when choosing a treatment program.

Maintenance Therapy

Opioid addicts have a third treatment option: maintenance therapy, which is the use of medication to eliminate the craving of the drug. Maintenance therapy is limited to treatment of opioid addiction, mainly heroin, but it can be used to treat addiction to OxyContin and other prescription pain medications. Maintenance therapy uses a medication within the same class as the addicting drug to prevent intoxication and withdrawal. This is very effective at eliminating the use of heroin and opioids and decreasing medical problems such as hepatitis C and HIV infection. The most common medication used for maintenance therapy is methadone, which can only be obtained at methadone clinics.

What Happens in Treatment?

The goal of addiction treatment is more than staying off the offending substances. When addiction becomes the focus of a person's life, it overshadows all other aspects of life: physical, mental, family, and social. For this reason, a multidisciplinary approach is used for addiction treatment.

The problems extend beyond the use of the drug. Addicts consistently numb themselves with drugs, which limits their ability to witness the whole tragedy. This is more than denial. It is compulsive drug seeking, beneath the level of conscious thought, driving them to continue to use despite the consequences. This is why treatment programs must assess and provide care for addictive behaviors and related problems to ensure recovery.

A Thorough Evaluation

A thorough initial evaluation determines whether addiction exists, the extent of the addiction, any other medical or psychiatric problems, and whether medical detoxification is necessary. Most treatment programs use psychological tests and a psychological evaluation to examine whether any mental health problems need to be addressed. Psychiatrists are available for evaluation and care of significant psychiatric illness. All of the evaluations are pulled together to form a treatment plan.

Good treatment provides the necessary care at the right time. Some of the problems, like detoxification, need immediate attention. Other problems, such as an addictive lifestyle, must be addressed during treatment. Still other issues, such as the healing of a family, require attention both throughout the treatment experience and afterward.

Detoxification

Some people confuse detoxification with treatment itself, but detox is only the beginning. Detoxification is a medical procedure used to prevent withdrawal symptoms and provide a safe and comfortable transition to a drug-free state. Detoxification differs by the class of drug that has been used and is often complicated by the regular use of more than one drug. For example, someone who uses alcohol and heroin would need separate, but simultaneous, detoxification from both.

Eliminating the drug from an addict's system creates extreme vulnerability to relapse because craving is incredibly strong at that point. After detoxification, the long-term changes to the brain of the addict and psychosocial problems must be addressed.

How Recovery Begins

Addiction treatment consists of therapy, education, and fellowship to address addictive behaviors, help the individual recognize the problems in his or her life, and provide the skills to address these problems and maintain abstinence.

Group Therapy

In group therapy, people are able to see in other addicts the very issues they cannot admit to themselves. This breaks down defenses and opens people's minds to the possibility that they are actually experiencing the same problems they see in others. The focus of group therapy is on abstinence, but because addicts experience deterioration in so many aspects of life, the groups deal with a wide variety of topics, including

• the physical consequences of addiction

• how alcohol and other drug use affected the family

• honesty

• how to use the support of others to address new problems

• how to deal with the losses caused by addictive behavior

Individual Therapy

Individual therapy is also used in addiction treatment. Each client is assigned a counselor who provides guidance and insight into addictive behaviors and the activities associated with healing in early recovery. These counselors are often, but not always, in recovery from addiction themselves. Counselors actually act as role models for the changes their clients need to make to start living drug free.

Individual therapy may also be needed to address private issues and certain mental health problems. If someone is having flashbacks of sexual assault or is extremely depressed, an individual therapist with specific expertise in trauma or mental health issues is critical. This level of psychotherapy requires a psychologist, psychiatrist, or social worker.

Education

In treatment, patients are educated about addictions as a brain disease, what to expect in early abstinence, and how to re-enter the real world. Lectures and reading assignments give people in treatment a clear understanding of the problems they are facing.

Fellowship

Fellowship plays an integral role in the treatment process as well. People in the midst of addiction treatment and in early recovery need help from each other—they may be the best teachers and role models for what works and what does not. The fellowship experienced in a treatment setting provides a level of intimacy that may have become foreign to the addict. They need to re-establish intimacy and positive relationships. They need the acceptance, understanding, and experience of another addict as a sounding board for their shame, guilt, and fears.

Residential Schools

When an alcoholic or addict is high school age, a residential school may be the best treatment option. You live full-time at a residential school, like a boarding school. The school is highly structured and constantly supervised.

In addition to an academic program, therapeutic residential schools have a staff of therapists, psychologists, and psychiatrists. Substance abuse and recovery education are taught, as well as special courses in independent living and coping skills. Some schools offer outdoor therapy programs that build character and emphasize self-esteem.

Other features of a therapeutic residential school include the following:

• Group counseling

• Individual counseling

• Organized physical activities

• Tutoring

• Twelve Step meetings

• Vocational training

Residential schools are a good choice for students who need a longer amount of time in a structured environment than a regular inpatient recovery facility allows. School sessions usually last from nine to twelve months, giving students time away from family tensions, enabling relationships, or other problems that can make recovery at home more difficult.

There are many different schools and philosophies about care and treatment for young people with drug problems. Try to get referrals from your inpatient treatment provider or a trusted professional. Ask about the clinical research on which any particular school's drug treatment program is based. If the program directors are less than forthcoming, you and your family might want to keep looking. ■

5

One Day at a Time

GETTING CLEAN AND SOBER

There's no single method or time frame for finding sobriety. For some of us, recovery happens from one day to the next. For others, it takes one minute at a time for days, weeks, or even months until we finally get it: we are either going to get clean, go insane, or die. »

THIS SOBRIETY SPONSORED BY ROGER

Years before, I'd met a guy named Roger, whom I knew had been sober for a long time. I also knew he had a copy of the book *Alcoholics Anonymous,* known affectionately as the Big Book. Since I figured I should read that book, I called him. He lent me his copy, started taking me to meetings, and told me stories of what it had been like for him, and what it was like now after nine years of sobriety.

Roger asked me if I had a Twelve Step sponsor, someone to guide and support me along the road to recovery. I didn't. Roger said he'd take the job, but only if I was willing to go to any length to do what it took. I was desperate, so I said yes.

Roger helped me develop a schedule and pattern of behaviors to follow, like living simply one day at a time. I went to ninety Twelve Step meetings in my first ninety days. I learned to call Roger and other sober people when I needed help, felt like using, or just got frustrated about little things in daily life. I learned to lose the phone numbers of my using friends, who ignored me anyway once I stopped frequenting the bars and selling them drugs. I quit my bartending job and started to look at the destruction—from unpaid taxes to ruined friend-ships—that addiction and I had left in our wake.

Some of this was torture, and at times I struggled to live one minute at a time without drinking, snorting a line, or slugging somebody. But before long, the Twelve Steps and the fellowship in those meetings started to sink in and make sense to me. I remember feeling completely awed by the unthinkable accomplishment of staying sober for seven straight days. I hadn't been sober that long since I was in junior high. Many Twelve Step groups give medallions, pins, or chips to mark significant sobriety milestones. When I got my thirty-day chip, I felt I could conquer anything and that my life was starting to finally fall into place.

There were voices in my head screaming at me to start using again to relieve the pain of everyday life and of past memories, resentments, and regrets.

Still, there were voices in my head screaming at me to start using again to relieve the pain of everyday life and of past memories, resentments, and regrets. Sometimes I felt like I was living inside a kaleidoscope, barely present in or able to see the world around me. At the same time, I knew I needed to be in a Twelve Step fellowship, because it was—for the first time in my life—a place where I felt I truly belonged and where others truly understood me.

Instead of my "special" drink, I had my "special" seat at the K Street meeting. I was eager to get back there, hang around before and after meetings with other sober folks, make coffee, empty ashtrays, and chat endlessly while sprawled comfortably on the trashy secondhand furniture in my new home away from home.

Artists who paint have a term called "gradation hue." At 100 percent gradation, all color is blotted, foggy, black, and indistinct. At 90 percent gradation, the color becomes less and less black, and the fogginess begins to lift. During my early days of sobriety, I felt like my mind moved from 100 percent gradation to 90 percent. In the years since, the color and texture of my life have become even clearer. Granted, the gradation hue still goes up and down, but it is almost always in a range far below 90 percent.

BABY STEPS

Life outside of meetings kept on happening, of course. Even though our romance was over, Andrew was thrilled with the positive change he saw in me. I needed to make amends to Andrew for a great many things, and I tried my best to do that. Most of all, I felt (and still do) deep gratitude toward Andrew for how he stood by me and firmly pushed me toward the help I needed.

Ongoing life also required money and a routine. I finally understood that bartending was no longer a good career choice. So I signed on with a temp agency and quickly landed a gig at a dot-com telemarketing company where I excelled. I got a second job at a coffeehouse on weekends, so I had something healthy to do every day. I went to the gym regularly so that I was feeling better in my body and releasing some natural-high endorphins.

Perhaps most significant, my creative ability to paint exploded. Suddenly I was open to my creative vibe. All the negative energy consumed by using seemed to transform into constructive energy that I could throw into my work. I became very productive and the more time I put in, the clearer the creative process became. Images seemed to construct themselves onto the canvas, conveying emotions so clearly.

With so much new work in my portfolio, I started walking it around town and showing it to galleries. Finally, a collaborative gallery called Infinity in the South End agreed to include a handful of my paintings in a group show. And they sold! A few months later, Infinity featured my work in a three-person show. Seeing my family, including my great-grandmother, at the opening reception was a significant moment in my new sobriety.

This sounds like a radical transformation because it was. Rather than living my life locked in a room with no windows,

Elite Player, Extreme User

MARTHA • FORT WORTH, TEXAS

■ MARTHA'S STORY CONTINUES FROM PAGE 81 ■

It took several months in treatment to get some hope and to begin believing maybe I could live sober and be happy. I did exactly what they wanted me to do, although I kicked and screamed a little. I wanted to leave many times, but by the grace of God, I didn't. At the end, they said I was going to a halfway house in Rochester, Minnesota. I was ticked—didn't they know I was a southern girl and liked my heat? But I went to the halfway house in cold Minnesota.

In previous treatments, my willfulness fought almost everything that was recommended for me. This time, somehow, I didn't resist. That's part of why I'm sober—I didn't do what I wanted, but what I was told to do. I was told to live in Rochester for a year, get a job, and attend meetings. I did it.

I worked in a bakery and it was humbling. Of course, I wanted to tell people who I used to be, where I went to school, that I was a soccer star who played alongside famous names; I was going places, I was smarter than they were, and on and on and on. But I kept my mouth shut and experienced a job and situation where I wasn't the best or most skilled. Other people were better at the bakery skills, and I learned that that was okay. I wasn't the best employee there, and it was great for me to still have to ask how to use the cash register. I was free of having to be someone who had to live up to what my ego told me to be—either the best or the lowest.

I connected with a sponsor and plenty of meetings. I did a genuine Fourth and Fifth Step, which was a real eye-opener. I learned how to depend on my sponsor, prayer, and the program. I moved from the halfway house into a house in Rochester with some friends. I got back in touch with my family, slowly rebuilding those relationships. I worked on doing the best I could at work, getting up and going faithfully every day.

Along with the freedom came some hard times when I wanted to quit and run out the door, screaming, "Don't you know I'm better than this?" But I stuck it out. That's where change happened—sticking to commitments, going to meetings, doing what I promised to do.

After a year, I went back to Fort Worth. I never dreamed that I could be really content and sober. My main fear was that without drugs, I couldn't be happy and free. But even though there were (and still are) hard times, I was able to be at peace. I rejoined the warmth and affection of my family, and now I can't imagine not calling or spending vacations with them.

■ MARTHA'S STORY CONTINUES ON PAGE 119 ■

I finally connected to the miracle of my own life and saw the unlocked doors available to me. Recovery gave me (and still does) the sight to see new hallways and rooms on the other side of the door—spaces in which I could actually experience my life. The alternative was (and still is) staying trapped by fear in the dark, locked room—drunk and high until I committed suicide or died of an overdose.

It took a lot of hammering and a long time to break through my wall of denial. Fortunately, a solution was around the corner, a solution available to any addict or alcoholic, no matter how young or old. Paradoxically, the solution is a lot of fun as long as we don't lose sight of the fact that recovery is only a reprieve from our disease.

CURE IT, DOCTOR

When I was on *The Real World,* my roommates asked a lot of questions about my addiction, how it worked, and what it meant. I was still very new in sobriety and afraid to talk about it. I also didn't have the clearest answers because I was still learning a lot of that stuff myself.

One thing they had a hard time grasping was that I would never get over or beyond my addiction to reach some point where I'd be "cured" and able to drink "normally" again. That's a hard concept for a lot of people to wrap their minds around. After all, we live in an age of many medical miracles. Surely some scientist, psychiatrist, or doctor has come up with a cure (or at least an immunization) for addiction? Well, not yet.

The fact is that *chemical dependency,* the term that includes both alcoholism and drug addiction, is a progressive disease that can't be cured. It can only be *arrested*—stopped in its tracks—through drastic, fundamental changes in the addict's attitudes and behaviors. Like me, most recovering alcoholics and addicts find the tools to make those radical changes in Twelve Step programs.

In practical terms, being chemically dependent means that if I were to take a drink of alcohol or snort a line of cocaine tomorrow, two things would be true:

1. It is very unlikely I could have only "a" drink or snort; I would have many and get trashed.

2. Within a fairly short time (hours, days, weeks, or months), I would be using at the same levels and engaging in the same reckless behaviors I did on the day I had my last drink.

That's why doctors and addiction treatment professionals say that the disease is arrested, not cured. If I start using again, I won't be back to that day in the woods where I had my first Jim Beam. Instead of starting from square one, I'd start in the South End, where I left off—drinking a dozen martinis and inviting strangers home who begged me to urinate on them. For me and many other sober alcoholics and addicts, it is important to remember that there is no cure. That's why we refer to ourselves as "recovering" rather than "recovered" from alcoholism or drug addiction.

For me and many other sober alcoholics and addicts, it is important to remember that there is no cure.

I possess an always active, thinking mind. That's a blessing some days and not so much on other days. Early in sobriety, my frenetic brain tried to understand the nature of alcoholism. It asked questions like, "Why me? Can I trace it all to genetics? Or was it all because of how I was raised, or some other factor?" As time passed, I realized that those questions weren't all that important or relevant—at least not to my recovery. But the process of questioning helped me start seeing my addiction as an entity separate from my self. That meant it was actually possible to start thinking of myself as a good and decent person—not easy for an addict!

Another important truth I learned from fellow recovering addicts is that my emotional development was arrested during my formative years when I started drinking compulsively. I got sober in a twenty-three-year-old's body and life, but in many ways I was only equipped with the emotions and relationship skills of a twelve-year-old. I had a lot to learn, and quickly.

EXPERTS

For me, it was important to attend a lot of Twelve Step meetings at the beginning because that's where I found the expertise on staying sober. I was surrounded by people with the same problem I had—but they laughed, had a good time, talked about solutions, and seemed to deal with life calmly and enjoyably. That motivated me to learn more about the Twelve Steps and shorthand slogans from the fellowship.

Concepts like *Keep it simple, First things first,* and *One day at a time* started coming up in my everyday conversations and sinking into my thought processes. I became more dependable and my life started to make more sense when I lived in twenty-four-hour periods, rather than getting caught in the trap of regretting the past or obsessing about the future. I also started to feel a Higher Power in my life and came to believe that there really was a force in the universe that wanted me to live, be useful to others, and experience peace.

At first, giving up old behaviors—like clubbing with one-time friends—looked like a boring path toward a boring life. But I was close enough to the misery of my using to try it anyway. I understood what an old-timer meant when he told me, "If you hang around the barbershop long enough, you'll eventually get a haircut." Staying away from the club scene and active addicts seemed like a smart move.

But I still had to battle my pride, ego, fear, and willfulness. For example, I became very judgmental toward my using friends, certain that my sixty days sober made me expert enough to diagnose their problems and look down on their failures to get clean. I piously condemned their intelligence, but my reactions were really all about me. I was simultaneously selfish and afraid with this new life I was choosing each day.

During my first three months clean and sober, I saw my good friend Frank regularly at the gym. I knew that Frank's addictive drug use was self-destructive and that I couldn't be around him a lot. Following my sponsor's advice, I tried praying for him and detaching with love from what the disease was doing to him. But my overblown pride also made me think that I could fix him and get him sober.

One day, I stopped by Frank's house to find him having an episode of traumatic, childlike outbursts. He'd apparently gone overboard on GHB, another drug he was abusing. I couldn't make sense of his reaction or get through to him. So I called an ambulance and went with him to the emergency room, where they pumped his stomach. Afterward, I suggested rehab and therapists, saying I wanted him to have a taste of the good sobriety I had: "Every thirty days clean would make a huge difference." It was painful to watch a friend go through the agony of addiction, knowing full well that there *was* a way out of his dilemma.

When I talked about the experience during a meeting that night, people reminded me that it wouldn't help Frank for others to tell him that drugs were causing his dilemma. Unless he admitted *he* was powerless over his addiction, nothing would change. I couldn't make that decision for him. All I could do was share my own story and then let go. Putting Frank's needs before mine and trying to argue him into sobriety simply wouldn't work. And it wouldn't be healthy for my sobriety.

It was painful to watch a friend go through the agony of addiction, knowing full well that there <u>was</u> a way out of his dilemma.

Sadly, Frank never did get to that first step of admitting that his addiction controlled him and that his life was unmanageable. He was thirty-nine when he committed suicide.

Fortunately, I found a lot to appreciate in my first weeks and months of sobriety. A memorable early gift was the invitation to speak at a Twelve Step meeting after being clean for ninety days. I trembled and stumbled as I told my story of what it had been like, what had happened, and what it was like now.

It felt like nothing I said made any sense, but people listened respectfully. I looked out and saw someone in the audience nod his head as if he knew exactly what I was talking about. I was amazed that I could tell my story in front of a group and that others seemed to take something useful from what I had to say. Several people, including a couple of newcomers, came up afterward to thank me and comment on the talk. That was unbelievable! I felt popular, accepted, and appreciated. It seemed I was finally making a real contribution instead of merely sitting and taking from other people in the program. I fell even more in love with Twelve Step members because we listened to each other and helped each other, and our efforts really mattered.

BREAKFAST WITHOUT BLOODY MARY

At one meeting, I heard Thomas, a twentysomething man with six months of sobriety, tell his story. I connected with what he said and we talked afterward. Thomas hung out with another good, young, sober guy named Randy, and I became friends with them both. We'd meet up before a meeting and grab something to eat afterward.

Pretty soon the three of us were having brunch together every weekend. We mostly talked about meetings we attended and people we met there. We bitched about some folks, but we were steadily building a friendship in which we could bounce things honestly off each other.

The Devil's Drug
CHARLIE • KNOXVILLE, TENNESSEE

I am twenty-two years old, but sometimes I feel as though I am forty or fifty. I am a recovering methamphetamine addict. I admitted myself to a rehabilitation facility, which was the best decision I have ever made in my life. The depression, anxiety, paranoia, memory lapses, and loss of self-esteem associated with the discontinuation of using meth are by no means worth any high or rush I ever had while I was on it. I now take antidepressants and sleeping pills, prescribed by a doctor, on a daily basis because of the damage I have done from abusing.

My distorted thought process while on meth has stayed with me. In rehab they told me that I would never get everything back that I had lost, memory-wise. The cravings never go away, despite all the negativity they bring. The drugged memories never go away, the nightmares never stop, and the self-confidence rebuilds more slowly than you can imagine. Methamphetamine is a drug of the devil—I wouldn't wish it on anyone. Staying up for one-hundred-plus hours while having "fun" eventually yields an addiction that will remain with you forever. I hate this drug, and if I had the chance to go back to the first time I ever tried it, I never would have taken that first hit.

Brunch wasn't always serious. Laughing over our respective romantic escapades, I used to joke that we were a pale-male version of *Sex and the City*. It was surreal to be eating breakfast with someone without a drink in my hand. I'd never experienced this before in my adult life. Our brunches confirmed that I no longer needed a Bloody Mary to feel good on a Sunday morning. In fact, those Bloody Marys had been just methods of getting me through a hangover. Today's brunches with Thomas and Randy were genuine fun—and I was awake and aware enough to notice!

However, even in those social situations, I sometimes struggled with feeling awkward. Without that glass crutch, I felt like an incomplete person, when what I really wanted was to feel just plain normal. I realized again that my formative years had been wasted by my being wasted. I'd been so stunted by drugs and alcohol that I had to learn how to be social from scratch; I had to learn to live life again.

CHANNELING MARTHA STEWART

During the first few months of sobriety, my living situation wasn't the best. I still lived in the rundown house with my estranged roommates—who did a lot of drugs and drinking. So I spent most of my time away from the house, working, visiting the gym, going to meetings, and socializing with program people.

One day, I decided to take advantage of the kitchen for something other than microwaving K. I would make dinner for myself instead of getting the usual takeout. I bought preskinned and preboned chicken breasts and vegetables. I carefully prepped the chicken by cutting it into small, uniform pieces. I steamed some of the vegetables and threw the rest in a pan with the chicken, stir-frying with olive oil. It was a bit like Martha Stewart meets Betty Crocker meets Chef Boyardee, but preparing that meal felt like the coolest thing anyone had ever done.

I was incredibly proud of this amazing feat and bragged about it widely. When my friends asked, "What did you do this weekend?" I beamed and answered, "Worked out at the

gym, did two shifts at the coffee shop, and cooked chicken!"
I laugh about that story now, but in some ways my stir-fry
excitement symbolized how little things were starting to
have more meaning and bring me satisfaction—even joy. In
sobriety, life felt simple, fine, and uncomplicated. And it got
better and better over time.

> It was a bit like Martha Stewart meets Betty Crocker
> meets Chef Boyardee, but preparing that meal felt like
> the coolest thing anyone had ever done.

I started to take care of myself because it felt good, not
because of some guilt-ridden set of silly rules. I used to go to
the gym and work out just to justify going out later in the
day to get drunk. I thought, "Okay, I'll suffer and work hard
on doing something good for me now, so tonight I can pay
myself back by getting wasted."

Now the gym became an important part of recovery. It
was a place where I could care for my body and help it
bounce back from the abuse it took while I was using.
Working out no longer seemed like a chore I had to do to
"earn" the reward of a drink. It felt great and fun on its own,
and I felt better physically, emotionally, and spiritually.

The biggest spiritual and emotional growth came from
going to meetings and working my way through the Twelve
Steps with a sponsor. Between work, the fellowships, getting in shape, and stopping the intake of poisonous chemicals,
I established a pretty healthy lifestyle. I felt inordinately
happy in my first few months of sobriety and went out of my
way to be fruitful and excited: painting a lot, selling my art,
getting a raise at work, and actually making eye contact
with, being interested in, and conversing with other people.
I often felt completely on top of the world, and I sometimes
went overboard living on my little pink cloud. But on the
days when I crashed into depression and resentment, my
sponsor and sober friends were there to help me through.
The end result was the ability to start learning how to bring
balance into my life.

FINDING THE REAL WORLD

Among those I made eye contact and friendly conversation with were two young women on the staff at my gym. One day when I came in, they said, "We've been dying for you to get here. Some people stopped by and posted notices about auditions for *The Real World* on MTV. You've gotta promise us you'll go, because we're sure you'll get the gig!"

The Real World was of the first reality television shows. Each season took seven people from different walks of life and gave them one place to live together in for four months. Their interactions and their private lives were filmed around the clock.

I looked at the audition date for *The Real World*'s eleventh season and said no way, because I had to work that day. Work was more important to my sobriety and life than being on any reality show. The young women kept encouraging me anyway, and that weekend I talked to my sponsor about it. He thought I now had what it took to keep first things first going through an audition, so why not try it? I got up enough courage to call my boss to ask for the time off, and he was cool with it. Everyone was supportive, so off I went.

I laughed when I got there—the auditions were being held at a gothic S and M club where I used to drink and buy drugs. The place looked lousy in the light of day, and the whole atmosphere, with dozens of kids trying to get on this TV show, was pretty absurd. So I decided to not take the scene too seriously, just be open and awake for the experience, and then go back to work and my normal life the next day.

As a result, I was more relaxed and carefree than most of the other people auditioning. I sat in a group of twelve while a really fun production assistant asked us questions about sex, religious beliefs, drugs, friendship, and other topics. I went happily home. To my surprise, the producers called me to come back the next day for a more in-depth interview, during which I told them everything about my drugging and recovery. They called me back again for the following day to videotape an interview. Then they started calling my friends and family for references on my character. Within a few weeks, they'd flown me to Los Angeles to sign a contract and announce I was a finalist.

Up until then, I hadn't watched *The Real World*. I started to tune in, and then fantasized about being sent to live in a house in Paris or London. The location didn't really matter, because I regretted not ever going away someplace for college, and thought anyplace would be a good chance to experience life outside Boston.

Then one day a producer called to say that I got the job and that I had eleven days to move to Chicago, where I'd spend the next four months living in a loft apartment with six other young people—none of us ever having met before. I yelled out in excitement and called all my friends, but at the same time I was thinking, "What am I going to do? How did I get myself into this?"

It usually isn't a good idea to make major life changes during the first year or so of sobriety. Newcomers are still learning how to live daily life without chemicals. But I felt I had kept my perspective throughout the audition process, laughing at some of the silliness and just being myself. Plus I really wanted a change of location in my life. I know now that this was not the wisest reason to make such a big decision early in sobriety, but I was stubborn—and, in the end, I was also lucky.

> **I told the producers that I had to be allowed to attend Twelve Step meetings and work privately with a sponsor, and that this was non-negotiable.**

Meanwhile, I went to work with my sponsor developing a plan for what I'd need in Chicago. I told the producers that I had to be allowed to attend Twelve Step meetings and work privately with a sponsor, and that this was non-negotiable. A Boston friend hooked me up with his Chicago friend, Jack, who promised to bring me to meetings and who quickly became my sponsor out there. On short notice, my sober buddies stepped right in and made sure my program bases would be covered.

Welcoming the Newcomer

ADAM • EAST GREENWICH, RHODE ISLAND

Enduring change is not a particularly strong suit of mine, especially during my early recovery. When I left the treatment setting to have another go at college, a lot of things changed in my life. One such change was living with a bunch of newly sober boys and girls who had a like interest in restarting, or beginning, college. The program making this possible was StepUP at Augsburg College in Minneapolis. I lived on a floor with about eight other guys and four girls.

I liked almost all of them and could tolerate very well living with them until one kid arrived on the scene during my third semester. He was a smart-ass. He was younger than me, yet his lack of shyness with others made him seem older. I, on the other hand, have always been cautious with new people and shy. I guess you could say I envied this guy's seeming ability to comfortably express himself and his ease in connecting with others.

At the time when he joined the floor house, I wasn't aware of my jealousy of his free-flowing nature. In fact, instead of admiring and respecting a personality trait I hoped to develop or look for ways to become less shy, I took it the other direction. I tore him down. I lifted the veil on his shortcomings and may have embellished some along the way.

I dismissed him as obnoxious and pretentious. I thought he was disrespectful toward others, especially those who had helped pave the way for the program to be established as it was at that time. I took his joking around with me (he joked around with everyone) as passive-aggressive behavior used as a means to "one-up" me.

Phew! I put a lot of effort into taking his inventory. I assumed it as a duty. Can you say "resentment"? In my experience, alcoholics are sensitive people or at least lacking emotional development. I consider myself an alcoholic of the "garden variety." The above illustrates just that. I had a tendency to pull down those who had skills or traits that I coveted.

It is funny, yet sad, how I had a penchant for pushing away those things that I desired. Why couldn't I have moved closer to those people and become familiar with them? Why not try to figure out what allowed them to express those skills that I envied, so I could try developing those things myself? No, the capacities to do such things are granted to those much less mentally tangled than me.

I also felt somewhat protected by my rebellious streak. I suspected that the producers chose me in hopes that I'd start using again during the taping and provide them with some drama. So I went into Chicago with a bit of "I'll show you!" in my step. I had nagging doubts about whether this decision was right for me, but I also felt a bit invincible. I figured if I had already found a way to stay clean and sober for five whole months, I could handle just about anything.

LIFE ON TAPE

When I got to Chicago, the first days were crazy, surreal, and extreme. Quiet and apprehensive, I opened the door to the loft and was blown away. On screen, you see a huge and stylish living space, but in reality the "loft" was a giant TV studio with hundreds of lights and dozens of cameras bolted in the corners and ceilings. I felt free, excited, joyful, grateful, afraid, uncertain, and desperate to cling to someone safe. I also knew without a doubt that I was about to start living in an elaborate fishbowl experiment.

For the first few weeks, I was scared and uncertain. Watching tapes of the early episodes, I see a deer-in-the-headlights look on my face most of the time. Then I adopted my "Mr. Counselor" role, asking probing questions of the other roommates or running emotional interference for them—in part to keep the focus on them and off me.

I don't know if I would have survived being part of some other *Real World* cast. My Chicago roommates addressed my deepest fears by accepting me for who I was rather than for who I slept with. The first day, we were all in the hot tub together when Aneesa mentioned that she is a lesbian. I felt an instant bond and grabbed her leg in excitement, feeling like a kid winning at hide-and-seek. As odd as the whole *Real World* scene was, I really loved all of my roommates. I was the oldest, and the others frequently came to me for advice and perspective. I felt trusted and confided in, like a true friend.

I took full advantage of my freedom to get away from the loft, go to Twelve Step meetings, and visit my sponsor. I bought a bike and rode it to meetings to lessen the odds of the cameras following me. I also took my time before coming back to the loft, hanging around after meetings for coffee or meals with sober friends. That was another way of keeping my head down in the line of fire that the cameras were shooting.

I didn't have my emotional force field up all of the time, though. The Human Rights Campaign (HRC), which promotes civil rights regardless of sexual orientation, held a fundraising banquet in Chicago, and I wanted to go. I also really wanted my roommates to come, so I started dropping hints. The others seemed to like me, and most at least mouthed support for gay civil rights, but they didn't initially take my hints. Finally, Kyle asked me directly, "Do you want us to come and show you support?" and I said yes.

That was an important lesson for me. Part of the adjustment I had to make from living drunk to living sober was unlearning the indirect behaviors (which were usually manipulative, if not downright dishonest) I was so accustomed to using. Meanwhile, I had to learn—and practice—new, honest, and more direct ways of interacting with myself and other people.

Part of the adjustment I had to make from living drunk to living sober was unlearning the indirect behaviors I was so accustomed to using.

Although he may not have seen it this way, Kyle's question forced me to be honest with myself and everyone else. I had to admit to myself that I wanted my roommates' support at the HRC event, where I wouldn't know anyone else and was afraid of feeling lost and lonely. I also realized that their attendance would give me concrete evidence that they really did accept me for who I was, rather than just give lip service. In the end, all but one of the roommates came and we had a good time.

Of course, looking back, it was a little childish to demand proof that my friends liked me. This story reminds me how I really was operating emotionally at the level of a middle-school kid during that time. Those old *Real World* episodes function as a video diary of my early growth in sobriety.

> My months working the Twelve Steps were starting
> to open my eyes to how compulsively judgmental I was—
> and how dangerous this was to my sobriety.

Theo was the only roommate who didn't attend the HRC banquet. That episode shows him calling his father to get assurance that he was making the right decision. At first glance, Theo and I seemed to have nothing in common. He had always been very close to his father, a Baptist preacher. He was straight, African American, and from the West Coast. His decision to stay home from the banquet, and other comments he made, told me that he'd never been around gay men before and had grown up homophobic.

In my drinking and using days, I wouldn't have given someone like Theo the time of day. Not only that, I would have trashed him to anyone who cared to listen. But my months working the Twelve Steps were starting to open my eyes to how compulsively judgmental I was—and how dangerous this was to my sobriety. So, I didn't dismiss Theo out of hand.

I loved how Theo kept it real. He seemed to be the only roommate who wasn't interested in gossiping about the others. When he and I were partnered up to construct sets for a Halloween show for the Chicago Park District, I could sense him rolling his eyes. I wasn't too sure about the arrangement, either. But once we started working together, I experienced Theo as an organized and responsible worker with a keen architectural eye. My sense for imagery, along with my painting ability, meshed perfectly with what Theo brought to the project. Looking at the other teams, we were grateful that we could count on each other. We both came away with mutual respect.

In reality, it took two or three weeks for us to become good friends. But on the TV show, it took fourteen weeks to show our friendship because the producers only had twenty-two minutes a week to tell our story and the stories of five other people.

Believe it or not, Theo is the only *Real World* roommate I still have regular contact with three years later. I didn't know about Theo's phone call to his dad until that episode aired on MTV, more than six months after the event itself. It hurt to watch, but he called me afterward and we talked about it. We admitted that each of us had said and thought some unkind and indefensible things during our four months together. I knew from that conversation, and subsequent ones, that our honesty with each other really had forged a solid friendship.

Life doesn't stop happening to us addicts just because we stop taking drugs.

That intense and sometimes painful experience taught me that I can't judge people by one moment in their lives. If every word you spoke over four months was videotaped and broadcast to the world, the odds are good that everyone you know could find at least one thing to be offended by—if they chose to be offended. The same is true for me and for Theo.

Most of us are blessed with people who love us enough to let our dumber comments and actions slide and roll off their backs. For my sobriety and spiritual growth, the key is what I choose to do in response to what other people say and do. Life doesn't stop happening to us addicts just because we stop taking drugs. Neither we nor other people suddenly become angels. We all remain sometimes appalling, sometimes magnificent, and mostly somewhere in between.

I think all seven of us on *The Real World: Chicago* eventually learned a bit of that lesson. When we watched the show air many months later, we realized that we had all, to one degree or another, grown beyond who we were during those four months of taping. In other words, we learned to let go and be grateful for what was, rather than to resent what wasn't.

As my time on *The Real World* came to an end, I was more comfortable around the cameras. The taping became a part of life that I didn't have to choose to control and resist, like I did at the beginning. Instead, I tried to have fun visiting Chicago's museums, enjoying its unique architecture, and exploring new things in a new city. That, along with many other positive and important experiences of those four months, never made it on the air. But that's life in "reality" TV land.

In my earliest clean and sober days, one of the most difficult things for me to believe was that I could ever enjoy life again. Could there possibly be anything fun to do or experience if I wasn't high? The answer surprised me.

Recovery

Continuing Care

A continuing care, or after-care, plan is for when your initial phase of treatment in a hospital or rehab is over. The process for choosing after care usually starts about day fourteen of primary care treatment.

Alcoholics Anonymous or Narcotics Anonymous meetings can be a critical part of continuing care, as are Al-Anon or Families Anonymous meetings for your family. (See page 115 for more on these programs.) In addition to Twelve Step programs, outpatient continuing care may include an extended care group, as well as an individual psychiatrist, therapist, or family therapist, depending on your case needs. Varying levels of continuing care options include the following:

- *Extended care* is similar to primary care treatment in a rehabilitation facility but with more attention paid to relapse prevention, behavior and lifestyle changes, family and relationships, and preparation for the outside world, including school and jobs. How long you stay in an extended care program depends on your needs, your circumstances, and your finances.

- *Halfway houses* are structured living environments with housemates also in recovery. The house manager is often a professional who has also been through recovery and can help residents stick to their recovery program. In a halfway house, the emphasis is on transitioning to the outside world, and residents work, attend school, or volunteer. Services of the halfway house may include individual counseling and group counseling, as well as Alcoholics Anonymous and/or Narcotics Anonymous meetings. Residents in halfway houses share chores such as housecleaning, cooking, grocery shopping, and laundry. Strict rules are part of any halfway house. A zero-tolerance policy means any resident who uses again is immediately asked to leave.

- *Three-fourths-way houses,* or sober houses, offer a sober living environment for those who do not need as much supervision as is found in a halfway house. The three-fourths-way house usually does hold Twelve Step meetings, but there is no twenty-four-hour staff or manager and you are responsible for your own meals.

Extended or continuing care programs are mostly run as nonprofit services. Insurance rarely covers the costs. On the other hand, expenses are about the same as what independent living would cost and sometimes include rent, food, utilities, counseling, and so on. Continuing care programs vary from one facility to the next, and programs may be defined differently from state to state, so be sure to ask specific questions about the halfway house or three-fourths-way house to understand the level of care the program offers. Residents stay at extended care or sober houses anywhere from three months to a year or more.

The Warning Signs of Relapse

People who care about you can usually see a relapse coming long before you actually pick up—but they are powerless to stop your downhill slide. If you stay aware and honest, there's a chance you can stop yourself in time. Keep an eagle eye out for any of the following red flags:

- Compulsive behavior
- Cutting back on or quitting Twelve Step meetings
- Defensiveness
- Denying your feelings
- Depression
- Feeling hopeless
- Feelings of arrogance
- Getting in touch with people who use drugs or abuse alcohol
- Going back to places where you used
- Increasing number of headaches, stomachaches, or other physical complaints
- Impulsive behavior
- Isolating
- Lack of fun activities
- Lying
- Nagging
- No daily routine/structure
- No satisfaction in work
- Not asking for help
- Overconfidence in your own recovery
- Under- or overeating
- Under- or oversleeping
- Overreacting to stress
- Self-pity
- Thinking you are "cured"
- Using over-the-counter medication (decongestants, pain relievers, cough suppressants) more frequently
- Whining

When you do notice these behaviors or attitudes, it's easy to twist your self-loathing and disappointment into an excuse for picking up. Don't! But don't be too gentle on yourself either. Remember the losses and pain your addiction caused, then take immediate action. Talk about your feelings to a healthy, trusted person; increase the number of Twelve Step meetings you're attending; if you've stopped a positive routine like exercise or volunteering, restart it; ask for help from a therapist, program friend, family member, or teacher.

Al-Anon

You don't necessarily have to be an alcoholic or addict to join a Twelve Step group. Al-Anon is for the family and friends of alcoholics. Al-Anon is based on the idea that substance abuse is an illness that affects everyone who comes into contact with it. The organization helps people accept that chemical dependency is a disease, educates them about the disease, and then offers tools for recovery. Most people who first join Al-Anon assume it's about fixing the addict or alcoholic in their lives. But Al-Anon is aimed at changing the attitudes of its own members and helping each other "recover" from being "addicted" to an alcoholic or addict.

Like AA or NA, Al-Anon uses a slight variation of the Twelve Steps and membership is free. Al-Anon is not group therapy, nor is it connected to any sect, denomination, political entity, organization, or institution.

At meetings, participants share stories, always trying to keep the focus on themselves rather than on the alcoholic or addict. Concepts such as codependence, detaching with love, and responding instead of reacting are discussed.

Al-Anon meetings for young people are called Alateen, although kids as young as ten may attend. An adult member of Al-Anon volunteers as a group leader for Alateen.

It also is quite common for those recovering from substance abuse to realize they, too, might benefit from attending Al-Anon meetings in addition to AA or NA. Often, they discover that they had alcoholic parents or grandparents. In Al-Anon, they can address how they have been affected by someone else's drinking or drug abuse.

You can find information and meeting locations by looking up Al-Anon in the white pages of the telephone book or by going to www.al-anon.alateen.org. ■

6

The Rest of Your Life

MAKING IT SAFE, SOBER, AND SEXY

Once you're clean and sober, you have to deal with the rest of your life. What do you do without those chemicals as the centerpiece—the only piece—of your day-to-day routine? It's not easy at first, but eventually, sooner than you think, you discover that the richness of the real world is beyond your wildest imagining. »

If I'd made a list of all the things I dreamed of doing and feeling on the day I finally got clean and sober, that list would look pathetic to me now. When I got clean, my imagination of what was possible in my life was still very stunted. The long list of what I have actually experienced during my few short years of sobriety is more than anything I could have imagined back in 2001.

OUT OF *THE REAL WORLD* AND INTO THE REAL WORLD

When my four months in the *Real World* loft ended, I had a healthy rhythm going for my life in Chicago. Through my sponsor and friends in recovery, I had a strong sense of safety and fellowship that I didn't want to leave. So I decided to stay in Chicago and work for the city, helping to run a kids' arts program in Garfield Park. Having lived all my life around Boston, I was taking a big step.

A few months later, the park district hired me to work on an exhibit by the well-known glass sculptor Dale Chihuly. I'd first seen his work when I was a teenager, and I had dreamed about studying it. Now I was meeting Chihuly and watching him work. I loved the excitement inherent in the process of glassblowing: the danger of the fire and the glass itself, as well as the intricate ways Chihuly wove brilliant colors together in his pieces. Seeing the work lit and installed resonated powerfully with me.

During the exhibit, I ran the Chihuly gift gallery and got valuable experience at managing my time and managing a small store. But the biggest gift was that other people trusted me to do those things. This was so different from anything I'd experienced drunk and high that I thought to myself, "I can't believe this is who I am." Even today I think those words, and I'm honored to have made so much progress. Sobriety has brought me to a place where responsible people believe in me, and I am worthy of their trust.

After leaving the MTV loft, I moved in with two sober friends. We asked each other for advice, spent cool time together, and enjoyed each other's company. This was radically different from my previous living situations. Other changes were obvious too: I had a salary and friends, and I paid my rent and other bills on time.

About six months later, as *The Real World: Chicago* air date got close, the show's publicity people cranked into full gear. After I did some promotional interviews and talks, talent agencies, public relations companies, and other people I didn't know started calling me. One of the calls was from an agency wanting me to model for them. That was something I wanted to try doing sober, so I went for it.

Sobriety has brought me to a place where responsible people believe in me, and I am worthy of their trust.

The center of the modeling world is New York City. Of course, it is also the center of the international art world, so I decided to make another leap and fulfill a dream of working as an artist in New York. The network of caring, sober friends jumped into action again. My Chicago sponsor, Jack, grew up in New York, so he gave me a list of meetings to go to and sober friends of his to meet. I didn't know exactly how everything would play out, but I knew that if I stayed sober, it would work out well.

Before I moved there, all I knew of Manhattan was the drug and party scene. I knew some drug dealers and had spent many weekends partying out of control at most of the city's nightclubs. The strong memories of being high in New York City now frightened me. Back then it was possible for me to get high anywhere. The difference now was that I had friends and meetings to help me make it okay, even though I was in a new place.

At first, I relied heavily on those healthy supports. But then I withdrew and started making some really dumb decisions. For example, I got into an unhealthy relationship with Stewart, an educated, unemployed, blue-eyed man with a distinguished British accent whom I'd met back when I was actively using. I was attracted by his charm and wit at first, but the relationship became a nightmare that I unwisely tried to fix by changing him and feeling lousy about myself—not worthy of something real and healthy.

Strangers recognized me from the TV show, and life became chaotic with distractions of interviews, parties, modeling jobs—all things that didn't have much to do with sobriety or painting. I felt that other people wanted a part of me and that I'd lost control of my life. Being an addict, my first instinct was to run away, rather than confront the problem. Instead, I ran deeper into the "celebrity" scene, glowing in the

Elite Player, Extreme User
MARTHA • FORT WORTH, TEXAS

MARTHA'S STORY CONTINUES FROM PAGE 98

In 2004, after four years away, I went back to Stanford as a twenty-five-year-old junior. My story was in some newspapers because I petitioned the NCAA to see if I could get some eligibility back. They said yes, and when I returned to school, I walked onto the soccer team. There was no scholarship, and I was the oldest one on the team by far.

I had put my ego aside as a "walk-on" and worked hard to get healthy and back in shape. That was a challenge because this was the same school and team where I'd been a star recruit. I'd been out of the sport for a long time, so my skills weren't as smooth and quick as before. I wanted to say, "I used to be this great player." But I knew that was my ego. Instead, I found people helping me, saying, "You'll get better. Be patient. You are who you are. Remember what you've been through." That was great to hear, because I still needed reminding that I could only live one day at a time.

MARTHA ■ CONTINUES ON PAGE 121

momentary limelight. I lost much of the spiritual strength and strong sense of who I became in Chicago because I wasn't putting sobriety first anymore.

THE REAL WORK STARTS

My sobriety honeymoon was ending, and the pink cloud was blowing away from underneath me. I heard Twelve Step friends say this was normal and the solution was to focus more on spiritual growth—and spiritual rewards. But I was seduced by the frenetic activity all around me. I tried to grab a bit of it all and ended up losing my healthiest drives and inspiration. My life felt like a stream twelve feet wide but only an inch deep.

Because of *The Real World,* I was invited to entertainment-industry award ceremonies. I felt like I'd been picked up and thrown, warp speed, into the strange la-la land of Hollywood celebrity. I introduced LeAnn Rimes at the Teen Choice Awards, and as I walked back to my seat, Britney Spears said, "Hello, Chris." She watched *my* show and knew who *I* was? How is this happening to me? I thought I was hallucinating, but I really wasn't.

**I was seduced by the frenetic activity all around me.
I tried to grab a bit of it all and ended up losing
my healthiest drives and inspiration.**

These experiences seemed very strange, but then, at the time, I had a press agent myself! All of this helped me realize that even the biggest celebrity is just another person, hyped up by publicity. I told myself the energy of Hollywood was too fleeting to be good for me. But as with drugs, that knowledge didn't keep me from getting caught up in its excitement.

I got more celebrity attention when the *Real World* producers had our cast speak on campuses around the country to promote the show. Of course, most of my talks centered on using and recovery, and soon I was being invited to lecture about this on my own, separate from the rest of the cast. My story was powerful, and I got better at delivering it. But I

It was so meaningful just to have that Cardinal jersey on. My parents were in the stands because they wanted to come. None of this happened when I was here before. I get tears in my eyes every time I stand on the field for the national anthem. I never thought it was possible to be back at Stanford, much less on the varsity. I am coping with the academic workload at a top-tier university, I have a major, and I'm slowly raising my grades. The whole experience is a miracle.

A rewarding part of my life today is helping other addicts and alcoholics. I've been given the gift of sharing my story with them, as well as with groups of young people. I have the restoration of so many important relationships. I am engaged again in my passion for hobbies, learning, sports, and other activities. My spirit was dead and my only passion was drugs and alcohol, but that is changed today. I know that if I picked up again tomorrow, all of my passion would immediately focus on getting high, with everything else going out the window. But now I have a choice.

At first, I thought sober life would be boring and dull day in and day out—that *mundane* that I hated so much. But I found that life in sobriety is more exciting than life using. I never know what's going to happen, good or bad. Unlike in my using days, I can feel the emotions; I'm present, aware, and awake. I can use friends to help me through the tough moments. In a way, that's not so different from the ways I used to use drugs to get me through. But by relying on good friends, I grow from going through my experiences, and something so rich comes from that. I used to think using was more fun than friends, and now I know it was just medication, part of having the disease of alcoholism. Relying on other people and my Higher Power, I have feelings for people, places, and things again.

There are hard times, but even life's battles are incredible if I pray, keep working my program, and have the right attitude. I can be present again on family vacations. I don't have to hide things, sneak off to use, or pretend not to be hung over. I wake up and every day is open and free for me to take care of my responsibilities and do the things I want and need to do. That's so much better than living completely preoccupied with waking up, getting in the car, and driving to find my dealer.

For today, I am free from the strangling grip of addiction. Of course, there are good days and bad days, but today I can say with certainty that life is full of so many gifts, so many opportunities, and so much beauty.

also slipped into playing the role of a person who was sober, rather than actually feeling sober. I started thinking I was better than other people because of all I'd "accomplished." Still, my speaking was a gift that helped keep me sober, even if I wasn't always in the best spiritual condition.

Back home, my everyday routine was comfortable enough, but I was barely going to meetings. I spent less time with sober friends and stopped praying. I kept telling myself that sobriety and my art were top priorities, but I kept putting other distractions first. Pretty soon I didn't care so much whether I was doing my best at sobriety or painting, so I half did them. It showed. I slipped into a scary, dangerous, and wishy-washy way of living.

My speaking was a gift that helped keep me sober, even if I wasn't always in the best spiritual condition.

Basically, I got complacent about the foundation of my new life, and I suffered the consequences. I was miserable. My time and energy were absorbed by people and places that "needed" me, like my next speaking appearance or modeling gig. I lost myself in the relationship with Stewart and began believing that it was everything to me. I started making irresponsible decisions again, like going on a vacation without having enough money for rent. I was careless.

The night before I was scheduled to speak at Yale, Stewart stayed out very late—and he was drinking. I was already a nervous wreck worrying about speaking at my first big Ivy League school—and now I wondered where the hell Stewart was. I finally went to sleep, and a couple of hours later, he came home drunk. I was furious and we got into a fight. He called me names, and filled with righteous self-pity, I shouted back, "How could you do this to me?"

I spent the rest of the night on an AeroBed and woke up the next day thinking, "I don't want to spend my time this way, and I don't want to be this unhappy anymore." That night, I gave an excellent lecture at Yale, one that connected strongly with the audience. At last, I realized that I really needed to put recovery ahead of everything else, especially if I hope to ever have anything else good happen in my life. I broke up with Stewart and started going to a lot of meetings again. I needed to fill up my misery and emptiness with something more substantive than flashes of fleeting celebrity.

I was lucky that I didn't relapse into drinking and using again. For years, I self-medicated my emptiness and pain with alcohol and other drugs, rather than examining why I felt bad and what I could do to change things. It is still difficult to separate myself from my sneaky, overblown egotism and, instead, work on nurturing my self-worth. I slip into the "poor-me" syndrome when I lose track of the Twelve Steps, slogans, and sober friends—and then start obsessing about the past and future, rather than living in the present.

Even in the celebrity limelight, I knew deep down that I'd much rather be known for my art, my work with young people, or other spiritually rewarding activities—things I'd be proud to sign my name to. I don't want my life reduced to being just a pretty boy on TV or a face in an advertisement. Celebrity attention can't feed my soul or make me into a useful, creative person. The good things only come when I apply the spiritual principles of the Twelve Steps, rely on my Higher Power, and do the next right thing—instead of doing some easy thing that inflates my ego.

SPEAKING OUT

Even as I struggled internally with the temptation of external validation, my speaking at colleges and high schools continued to expand and become more effective. Because I was on a popular TV show, I could be a vessel to carry the message of sobriety. That was a big responsibility.

Today, lecturing about addiction and recovery is an important part of my life and career. It is a privilege to be able to attract kids with my story of being on *The Real World,* and then have them come away with a deeper understanding of addiction and recovery. I am growing in awareness of what audiences are feeling, and I'm learning how to read the

Two Ways I Stay Sober

JACKIE • LOS ANGELES, CALIFORNIA

First, yoga. I do between an hour to two hours of yoga a day—at least I try to fit it into my schedule. I have to go early in the morning—not what I'm used to. The Bikram yoga is amazing. They heat the room to 110 degrees, and the class lasts for ninety minutes. You have never, ever sweated as much as you do in this class. It cleans you out—and the heat of the room warms your joints so you can stretch farther. Your skin looks fantastic all day long, and I love the tone in my arms that yoga builds!

Second, Venti House Blend. I bleed Starbucks.

energy between them and me. I work to recognize how emotionally exposed I can be and how open they are. Sometimes I connect and sometimes I don't; it seems to depend most on how willing I am to be personal and vulnerable.

Some of the most intense and satisfying moments of my life come through these talks, like the time a college student stood up holding a copy of the book *Narcotics Anonymous*. She announced that she had five days clean, and the whole auditorium erupted in applause. I realize my speaking only helps on a small scale, but it is important for people to know that recovery is possible, no matter where you are or how old you are.

My most memorable talk, however, was during a fundraiser for Fenway Community Health Center, where I'd gone for drug abuse treatment. I received a Visibility Award for being openly gay nationally on *The Real World,* and my celebrity helped the health center raise a lot of money. But, on a personal level, it was a thrill to be stepping up to take responsibility for showing gratitude to an organization and staff who gave me so much. Plus, my parents, sister, great-grandmother, and other family and friends were in the audience. That moment symbolized the strength and transformation sobriety gave me, and my effort to make amends for the hurt I had caused my loved ones in the room.

Making myself visible on the topic of recovery is a risk because I become a role model for some people. But I can't live on a role model's pedestal because I am still human, make mistakes, and could lose it all tomorrow by taking one little drink. My ego and pride don't get too overblown if I remember this stubborn fact. When I keep that knowledge front and center, my talks get better too. What a bargain!

DRUGS DON'T DISAPPEAR

Unless you choose to be a complete recluse, you can't live clean and sober without coming across regular reminders that drugs and alcohol are readily available. However, when addicts stay in fit spiritual condition, then we have very effective tools for dealing with this reality.

Here's an example. Sometimes when I drive past a billboard for some kind of alcohol, or see someone smoking pot, I'll flash back to rosy memories of using's pleasures. But I don't feel like I have to use, or I don't have a compulsion that I must wrestle to the ground. That's because I have options now. Through prayer and meditation, I've developed tools to deal with these temptations fairly easily.

When I have a using memory, it's as if the bird of addiction has flown into the barn of my mind. I don't necessarily have to combatively shoo the bird out the barn door. I calmly let it fly around, hitting its head on the walls, while I get on with the rest of my chores. If I leave the door open to a life without using and let the bird just be what it is, it will fly out on its own. I don't have to react by picking up a drink or snorting a line.

Oddly enough, the little chores and details of life are appealing to me now in a way they never were when I drank and used. In fact, I hardly even recognized them back then! Now I appreciate waking up every day, because I'm not struggling with a hangover or battling the shakes from being up for two days on meth. I enjoy smelling things, listening to music, and feeling intimacy with a partner, rather than feeling like making love is a dark and dangerous place.

I'm aware of the many small moments that make up life, like the sun on my skin or the expression on someone's face. I'm not perfect; not every day is filled with bright awareness. But I now know how to connect with life from my soul instead of being trapped in a vacant, selfish existence. Sobriety gives me the chance to grow daily.

A DIFFERENT KIND OF K

Recently, one of those chances appeared on my breakfast table. A friend introduced me to a cereal called Kashi GoLean Crunch. It is amazingly delicious and I became obsessed with it. Apparently I have a lot of company, because every time I buy a box, someone else in the store comments about it. In fact, I'm convinced there's an entire Kashi GoLean Crunch subculture out there!

I liked the cereal so much that I started eating it at all times of the day. One day when I was feeling lonely, I ate a box and a half in one sitting. I knew I was full, but I didn't feel full, so I kept on eating—trying to fill an emotional emptiness with a physical substance. Sound familiar? I soon discovered that my relationship with Kashi GoLean Crunch was not much different than it was with special K (not Special K, the competing cereal)—I couldn't eat just one bowl. I had to have two or three, at least.

I learned (or, more accurately, relearned) an important lesson. I can't be healthy if I'm not taking care of my deepest needs and longings.

However, I was able to go cold turkey from Kashi for three whole days. Then, walking home from the gym, I saw the Food Emporium across 14th Street. Like Pavlov's dog, I salivated as neon flashing images of Kashi GoLean Crunch invaded my mind. My obsession grabbed hold and the addict in me started talking: "How about some Kashi GoLean Crunch as a reward for your workout? It can't hurt to cross the street to the grocery and buy just one box, can it?"

So, I went in and bought a box. I went home and had two bowls, making sure to slurp up the sweet-tasting soy milk that the glorious cereal left behind in my bowl. I realized a terrible pattern was starting up again, but then I started creating rationalizations for keeping the pattern going. "If I mix it in with that twiggy, disgusting, sixty-calorie cereal, then I can have just a little. Or maybe I should start eating it in coffee mugs instead of bowls, to keep my intake down."

My Kashi GoLean Crunch habit got so crazy so fast that I brought it up in therapy and meetings.

I learned (or, more accurately, relearned) an important lesson. I can't be healthy if I'm not taking care of my deepest needs and longings. I certainly can't be healthy if all I eat is Kashi GoLean Crunch, any more than I was healthy when all I did was take drugs and drink. It is inevitable that loneliness will sometimes strike, so I have to recognize when it does and then apply the tools of sobriety to the situation: call people, go to meetings, feel the loneliness without compulsively hanging on to it, reach out so I'm not alone, and be of service to others.

In Twelve Step groups, we often use the word HALT to help us. When we feel *Hungry, Angry, Lonely,* and/or *Tired,* we are vulnerable to compulsive thinking and behavior. So, if I find my day filled with obsessions about getting to the gym, shopping, or even eating cereal, then it's time to halt and check my HALT status. Without fail, I'll find that I am hungry, angry, lonely, tired, or some combination of all of them. That's my signal to let go of the obsession of the day, and get the help that will really cure what ails me.

ART OF LIFE
When I look around my apartment, I see a thousand reminders of the rewards this manner of living brings. My place isn't fancy, and it might strike some people as bohemian. I have a large studio space, where I can (and do) work on numerous canvases at the same time. I have storage for my completed paintings, and I even have some work up on my walls. The place is organized, I have a bed, and the kitchen is clean. It's hard to imagine how different this is from the squalid places where I used to live.

Plus, my apartment/studio is surrounded by a vibrant city filled with galleries, other artists, and people interested in art. Art collectors have begun to commission pieces from me, which is a wonderful honor. Not to mention the excitement of meeting these collectors, traveling to their homes, and knowing that my painting can give them joy. It's beyond my wildest dreams.

I'm discovering that I'm still young in my art and have plenty to learn. Because of sobriety, I am more open to advice and mentoring from experienced artists. They encourage me to put my energy and focus into the paintings themselves. I get impatient sometimes because I want the world to see and enjoy my work. But most days, I give myself space and time to evolve and grow as an artist. It's hard to beat the feeling of sitting down with a blank canvas and fresh paints to let inspiration take me on the wonderful journey of creating something exciting.

Sobriety gives me tools to decide life questions with honesty rather than from fear.

It's been awhile since I've been involved in a serious long-term relationship. That's fine by me. While there are things about dating that suck drunk or sober, I enjoy most of my dating experiences. I'm meeting interesting people and feeling secure about putting my primary energies into becoming the kind of responsible, mature person who will eventually be a good long-term partner.

I've dated a man who says he would like to move faster toward a more committed relationship. He's a wonderful guy who lives an affluent and fascinating life. Despite the allure, I feel comfortable telling him I'm not ready for something more permanent. By being honest and making my limits clear, I act on being true to myself. Being true to myself means I must be truthful with everyone in my life, and that is a positive in most every relationship. The result is that, for now, we are enjoying each other as we are, without obsessing over an uncertain future.

As a practicing addict, my boundaries were nonexistent. I slept around voraciously. But all of that so-called intimacy didn't make me feel better. These episodes were out-of-control, compulsive attempts to fill a hole inside me. But just as I couldn't find enough cocaine to fill the void in my soul, I couldn't find enough sex or enough partners to do it, either. When I did enter longer relationships, I tried to force a huge, unrealistic commitment too soon. That defeated the purpose of being with someone—to steadily grow toward deeper intimacy with and knowledge of one another.

Sobriety gives me tools to decide life questions with honesty rather than from fear. I don't have to be afraid that I'll never find a perfect, permanent partner. With each new person I meet, I can learn and grow. If and when I arrive at "the" relationship, I want to contribute a whole person, rather than just 20 percent of me. Meanwhile, I can trust my Higher Power, knowing that this trust will bring me where I need to be and where I can be the most loving and useful. When I actually use the tools of healthy sobriety, I can feel my healthy boundaries and know that I am making progress.

MICROWAVE THANKSGIVING

For proof of sobriety's blessings, I think of last Thanksgiving, the first time I hosted members of my family for the holiday. If you saw how tiny

The Real World

DANA • PIGEON FORGE, TENNESSEE

I'm thankful for the strength that helps me build and rebuild real relationships with myself and with other people. Drugs seemed like a way out, a way to party the troubles away, a way not to care because that seemed like it would be easier. I'll be honest; sometimes it was fun. But it was a cruel illusion. The ups and downs are now more real. I can gain meaning from them. They're not just another hangover or withdrawal. Now, today, for me, this is the "real world."

my kitchen is, you may suspect that I fed everyone Kashi GoLean Crunch. But I didn't—I prepared a full-blown turkey dinner.

When I started out, I wasn't sure I could pull it off. Once I invited my mother, stepfather, and sister to Thanksgiving in New York, I immediately started to panic. My alarmist alcoholic mind started screaming, "You don't know how to cook! You'll need a caterer. It's too late to hire a caterer; they're all booked by now!" With a quick meditation, deep breath, and simple prayer, I was able to turn off the alarm and get to work.

I went to an organic market to buy more varieties of root vegetables than I knew existed. I made sweet potato pie and pumpkin pie. On Thanksgiving morning, I set my small table, put the turkey in my tiny oven, and started running baked potatoes, cooked yams, green beans, and what seemed like a dozen other side dishes through the microwave. It was starting to look like I was making a feast for fourteen instead of four. Once dinner finally started, it took me awhile to settle down, between my overall excitement and running back into the kitchen to make sure everything was perfect.

Finally, after the rolls were done and the turkey sliced, I settled down to relaxing and devouring the meal with my loved ones. In the background, the stereo played a soft jazz playlist I had downloaded from my iPod. There was my mother, all dressed up in the candlelight, enjoying a meal I had prepared for her. Instead of being high during another Thanksgiving at my grandparents' house, my family and I were surrounded by my paintings and my new, sane, quiet, and full life. My body tingled with gratitude and joy at the sight.

To have people over for dinner is deeply symbolic, and having my family for Thanksgiving was even more so. It shows that I am disciplined enough to do the simple and important things, and brave enough to overcome my fears of failing.

As I sit here looking around my living space, I wonder if I deserve it. My surroundings and my work have improved beyond what I could have imagined. So has my behavior. The smallest things prove the evolution. I can tell someone I'm going to a Twelve Step meeting, and I actually make it. If I'm going to be late, I call and take responsibility, rather than lying or making excuses. I am concentrated on my art and on the wonderful people in my sobriety communities.

I am proud of who I've become and humbled by how much of my progress is due to the power and efforts of others. I have choices and opportunities. Before sobriety, my only choices appeared to be dying or committing suicide in stages by continuing to use. Today, everything about how I perceive things is built on taking the First Step: admitting I am powerless over alcohol and drugs, and that my life is unmanageable without a Higher Power in it.

I am proud of who I've become and humbled by how much of my progress is due to the power and efforts of others.

Words are inadequate to completely explain what my using life was like, what happened, and how wonderful things are now. Not even the finest painting could do the job entirely. Nevertheless, I hope that you have found at least one thing of value in this book.

If you struggle with your alcohol or other drug use, have only nagging questions, or care deeply about someone trapped in addiction, here is my wish for you: understand that it *is* possible to live happy, joyous, and free. The effort and sacrifice may seem insurmountable, but it's worth any struggle to rejoin the fully living. Above all, know in some part of your being that there is hope. There really is. And for that I am deeply grateful.

Health
WHAT YOU NEED TO KNOW

Nutrition and Diet

Eating well is critical to anyone's recovery. Instead of putting addictive substances in your body, you can begin to focus on nourishing it. By paying attention to nutritional guidelines, you can have better energy, mental and physical strength, and good overall health.

Eat balanced, regular meals. Avoid snacking on junk food and simple carbohydrates that can cause rapid and intense fluctuations in blood sugar. You may actually crave alcohol or other substances in order to counter anxiousness or depression caused by low blood sugar. The brain chemistry of alcoholics or users may be especially sensitive to sugar, either because of genetics or alcohol and drug use. So trying to minimize sugar in your diet is essential to both recovery and your clean life.

Stay hydrated. Our bodies need water to function properly, yet we are constantly losing water through sweat and elimination. We need to replenish it by drinking eight glasses of water or other liquids a day. Otherwise, dehydration can lead to headaches, lack of concentration, feeling tired, and even kidney damage. If you've been abusing alcohol or other drugs, you may have been in a state of chronic dehydration, so your body really needs its eight glasses a day. Coffee and caffeinated sodas are diuretics that actually remove fluids from your body and do not count toward the recommended daily intake of liquids.

Get the nutrients you need. Eat a variety of nutrient-rich foods from all the food groups, paying particular attention to whole grains and fresh fruits and vegetables. Federal guidelines released in 2005, for example, recommend nearly doubling the amount of fruit and vegetables in our diet, raising the daily goal from five servings to nine, or about four and a half cups per day. Choose whole grains over processed, and vegetable oils like canola over hydrogenated oils used in processed foods. Ask your physician to recommend a vitamin or dietary supplement specific to your own health needs, especially in the early weeks of recovery.

The following nutrients are of special importance if you've been addicted to alcohol or other drugs:

Nutrient	Why You Need It	Where to Get It
B vitamins	Deficiency in thiamin (vitamin B_1), common in alcoholics, can cause the serious health condition known as Wernicke-Korsakoff syndrome; deficiency in B vitamin folic acid causes anemia.	Whole grain breads and cereals and complex carbohydrates such as brown rice
Calcium	Alcohol use depletes the body's store of calcium.	Milk, yogurt, calcium-fortified orange juice, cheese, salmon, sardines, broccoli, collard greens
Vitamin C	Helps heal damaged body tissue.	Oranges, grapefruit, tomato juice, blueberries, strawberries, kiwi, broccoli, brussels sprouts
Protein	Helps regulate blood sugar and heal damaged body tissue. If you have severe liver damage, ask your doctor about your best sources of protein.	Fish, lean meats, cheese, tofu, eggs, yogurt, peanut butter, nuts, high-protein pasta
Iron	Iron absorption is affected by alcohol, leading to a susceptibility of anemia in alcoholics.	Beef, garbanzo beans and other dried peas and beans, oysters, sardines, soybeans, tofu, spinach
Beta carotene	People who have abused alcohol and tobacco may have increased risks of certain cancers; beta carotene guards against cancer	Leafy green and yellow vegetables and fruits

Relationships in Recovery

Many a young person feels confused about sex. If you're also a young person in recovery, those feelings may be even more pronounced, especially if during the time you were using, your sexual behavior was either downright deadly or less than safe. You may be concerned about your reputation. You may have questions about your sexual orientation. Those concerns and questions are normal. When you're a teen, you begin to learn how to relate to people of the opposite sex and to develop your own sexual identity. But if you've been using as a teen, drugs and alcohol prevent you from developing a healthy sexuality and a healthy sense of self. Because you are not truly yourself when you're using, you can't possibly learn how to relate well with others.

It is recommended that adults in recovery not become involved in a sexual relationship for at least the first year of recovery, and the same is true for teens. You need time to reestablish a healthy life before you can make the emotional investment of an intimate relationship.

Practicing safe sex when you are clean gets you in the habit of safe sex, and being prepared with condoms, making them a part of your regular sexual practice, may help prevent sexually transmitted diseases, even in the event of an ill-advised sexual encounter.

Exercise in Recovery

Like establishing and maintaining a good diet, exercise is an important part of your recovery. You probably shouldn't begin training for a marathon in the early days of your recovery, but getting into the habit of exercise is a good first step. Regular exercise can improve your sense of physical well-being and help reverse the toll addiction took on your body. It improves your cardiovascular and circulatory capacity, increases your energy and endurance, builds and tones your muscles, and helps you attain an ideal weight. You sleep better, handle stress better, and the endorphins released in your body when you exercise will even help you think and focus more clearly.

You don't have to have been an athlete to start an exercise program in recovery—anyone can begin to exercise and improve health and strength. Just be sure to take it easy at first. Taking things to extremes is what got you into trouble in the first place. So it's not about the intensity of your exercise in the early stages of recovery; rather, it's about making and keeping a commitment to exercise for twenty minutes every day. Begin by taking a walk every day and work up to more vigorous forms or longer periods of exercise as your improving health allows.

Make it regular. To increase your chances of making exercise a regular habit, establish a schedule you can stick to. Morning, afternoon, evening— it doesn't matter when you do it; it only matters that you choose a time that's convenient and do it around that same time every day.

Make it fun. You're more likely to stick with an exercise program you enjoy. If your exercise regime is challenging enough for you, you'll look forward to doing it every day. You may choose a single form of exercise, such as yoga or jogging or bicycling, but you can keep it interesting by varying your workout to include different types of classes or different routes. You can also mix up your activities, taking a bike ride on Saturdays, a yoga class on Tuesdays, and jogging every other day. Some people exercise with a friend or a partner to make it more sociable and supportive. The idea is to make sure you're having fun so you don't get in a rut and lose interest in exercising.

Make it doable. If a gym membership is too expensive or the gym is too far away to be convenient, exercising on gym equipment is just not realistic. So choose an exercise activity that suits you. If you only have thirty minutes a day you can devote to exercise, taking a class you have to get back and forth to is impractical. Use at-home class tapes (such as the many yoga and Pilates programs available), or choose an outdoor activity like walking, running, or biking that you can do right from your front door. You can even set up a little home gym, with simple equipment such as weights and a jump rope. Check what activities are available and appealing to you and how much time and money you can devote to them, and then choose accordingly. Because if it's not doable, it won't get done.

Make it safe. Consult a doctor before beginning an exercise program. Your doctor knows the state of your general physical health and can help guide you to the amount and type of exercise that your body can handle to start with. Drink plenty of water before, during, and after your workout to stay hydrated. Wear comfortable clothing, do gentle stretches before and after exercise to prevent injury, and gradually increase the amount and intensity of your exercise to avoid soreness and injury.

Make it moderate. Overexercising can lead to injury, and that can halt your fitness goals indefinitely. Also, it's easy for exercise to become a replacement for other work you should be doing in recovery. Working out is great, but it's a kind of solitary, personally absorbing activity. Working on your relationships or other issues in recovery should always take priority over exercise. In a worst-case scenario, exercise can even become an addiction in itself. If you find you are focused on exercise over your recovery, your job, your relationships, or other obligations, it may be a problem you will have to address along with your primary addictions. ■

Resources

Hazelden Foundation
(800) 257-7800
www.hazelden.org

**Information on Addiction
and Treatment**

National Clearinghouse for Alcohol
and Drug Information
(800) 729-6686
www.health.org

National Council on Alcoholism
and Drug Dependence
www.ncadd.org

National Institute on Alcohol Abuse
and Alcoholism
www.niaaa.nih.gov

National Institute on Drug Abuse
(800) 662-4357
www.nida.nih.gov
www.teens.drugabuse.gov

Regional Alcohol and Drug
Awareness Resources
(800) 729-6686

Substance Abuse and Mental Health
Services Administration (SAMHSA)
http://ncadi.samhsa.gov

Recovery Support

Alcoholics Anonymous
(212) 870-3400
www.alcoholics-anonymous.org

Cocaine Anonymous
(800) 347-8998
www.ca.org

Crystal Meth Anonymous
(213) 488-4455
www.crystalmeth.org

Narcotics Anonymous
(818) 773-9999
www.na.org

**Support for Families of
Alcoholics and Addicts**

Al-Anon/Alateen
(888) 425-2666
www.al-anon.alateen.org

Families Anonymous
(800) 736-9805
www.familiesanonymous.org

Nar-Anon
www.naranon.com

Smoking Cessation

American Cancer Society
(800) 227-2345
www.cancer.org

National Cancer Institute
(800) 422-6237
www.cancer.gov

**AIDS/HIV/Sexually
Transmitted Diseases**

Centers for Disease Control
National AIDS Hot Line
(800) 342-2437

National Center for HIV, STD
and TB Prevention
Divisions of HIV/AIDS Prevention
www.cdc.gov/hiv/dhap.htm

Medline Plus
www.nlm.nih.gov/medlineplus/
sexuallytransmitteddiseases.html

Sexually Transmitted Diseases
Hot Line
(800) 227-8922

Sources for "What You Need to Know"

Risk Factors

Genetics

Claudia Black, *Straight Talk from Claudia Black: What Recovering Parents Should Tell Their Kids about Drugs and Alcohol* (Center City, MN: Hazelden, 2003).

Your Family

Claudia Black, *Straight Talk from Claudia Black: What Recovering Parents Should Tell Their Kids about Drugs and Alcohol* (Center City, MN: Hazelden, 2003).

National Council on Alcoholism and Drug Dependence

National Clearinghouse for Alcohol and Drug Information

Mental Illness and Emotional Problems

New York Presbyterian Hospital, Payne Whitney Psychiatric Clinic

National Council on Alcoholism and Drug Dependence

National Clearinghouse for Alcohol and Drug Information

The Substances

Alcohol

National Council on Alcoholism and Drug Dependence

National Clearinghouse for Alcohol and Drug Information

National Institute on Alcohol Abuse and Alcoholism

Texas Department of State Health Services

Cocaine, Ecstasy, Heroin, Marijuana, Mescaline, Methamphetamine, Special K

Carol L. Falkowski, *Dangerous Drugs: An Easy-to-Use Reference for Parents and Professionals,* 2nd ed. (Center City, MN: Hazelden, 2003).

Drug Information Online

Focus Adolescent Services

Go Ask Alice! Columbia University's Health Q & A Internet Service

Hazelden Foundation

National Clearinghouse for Alcohol and Drug Information

National Institute on Alcohol Abuse and Alcoholism

National Institute on Drug Abuse

Office of National Drug Control Policy

Partnership for a Drug-Free America

Substance Abuse and Mental Health Services Administration

Turning Point Foundation

U.S. Drug Enforcement Administration

Alcohol Abuse Prevention at Virginia Tech

Washington State Alcohol/Drug Clearinghouse

Side Effects

Sex and Drugs

Al J. Mooney, Arlene Eisenberg, and Howard Eisenberg, *The Recovery Book*
(New York: Workman Publishing, 1992).

Planned Parenthood

Acne

Dan Kern, *Clear Skin: Heal Your Skin and End the Breakouts Once and for All*
(New York: Perigee, 2004).

Go Ask Alice! Columbia University's Health Q & A Internet Service

Al J. Mooney, Arlene Eisenberg, and Howard Eisenberg, *The Recovery Book*
(New York: Workman Publishing, 1992).

Smoking

John Slade, *Addressing Tobacco in the Prevention and Treatment of Other Addictions*
(New Brunswick, NJ: Saint Peter's Medical Center, 1998).

Terry Rustin, *Quit and Stay Quit Nicotine Cessation Program* (Center City, MN:
Hazelden, 1994).

Mountainside Foundation

Finding Help

Twelve Step Programs

Alcoholics Anonymous Web site (www.alcoholics-anonymous.org), literature, and interviews with members

Types of Treatment, What Happens in Treatment?, How Recovery Begins

Marvin D. Seppala, "How Addiction Treatment Works," in *When Painkillers Become Dangerous: What Everyone Needs to Know about OxyContin and Other Prescription Drugs* (Center City, MN: Hazelden, 2004), 31–64.

Residential Schools

Partnership for a Drug-Free America

Hazelden Foundation

The Family Foundation School

Academy at Swift River

Recovery

Continuing Care

Partnership for a Drug-Free America

Saint Vincent's Hospital Westchester, Maxwell Institute

Turning Point Foundation

The Warning Signs of Relapse

Hazelden Foundation

Conifer Park

Saint Vincent's Hospital Westchester, Maxwell Institute

Al-Anon

Al-Anon Web site (www.al-anon.alateen.org), literature, and interviews with members

Health

Nutrition and Diet

Hazelden Foundation

Al J. Mooney, Arlene Eisenberg, and Howard Eisenberg, *The Recovery Book*
(New York: Workman Publishing, 1992).

Relationships in Recovery

Go Ask Alice! Columbia University's Health Q & A Internet Service

Al J. Mooney, Arlene Eisenberg, and Howard Eisenberg, *The Recovery Book*
(New York: Workman Publishing, 1992).

Alcoholics Anonymous

Exercise in Recovery

Hazelden Foundation

Al J. Mooney, Arlene Eisenberg, and Howard Eisenberg, *The Recovery Book*
(New York: Workman Publishing, 1992).

Index

ABOUT THE AUTHOR

Chris Beckman is an artist who has had group and solo shows in New York and Boston, as well as participating in the Biennale in Florence. A former cast member of MTV's *The Real World: Chicago,* he also models and has been featured in ad campaigns for Polo/Ralph Lauren and the Gap, among many others. He speaks on addiction and recovery at colleges and high schools around the country. He currently lives and works in New York City.

For Chris Beckman speaking inquiries, please call
800-727-4571 or 800-328-0098.

Hazelden Publishing and Educational Services is a division of the Hazelden Foundation, a not-for-profit organization. Since 1949, Hazelden has been a leader in promoting the dignity and treatment of people afflicted with the disease of chemical dependency.

The mission of the foundation is to improve the quality of life for individuals, families, and communities by providing a national continuum of information, education, and recovery services that are widely accessible; to advance the field through research and training; and to improve our quality and effectiveness through continuous improvement and innovation.

Stemming from that, the mission of this division is to provide quality information and support to people wherever they may be in their personal journey—from education and early intervention, through treatment and recovery, to personal and spiritual growth.

Although our treatment programs do not necessarily use everything Hazelden publishes, our bibliotherapeutic materials support our mission and the Twelve Step philosophy upon which it is based. We encourage your comments and feedback.

The headquarters of the Hazelden Foundation are in Center City, Minnesota. Additional treatment facilities are located in Chicago, Illinois; Newberg, Oregon; New York, New York; Plymouth, Minnesota; and St. Paul, Minnesota. At these sites, we provide a continuum of care for men and women of all ages. Our Plymouth facility is designed specifically for youth and families.

For more information on Hazelden, please call **1-800-257-7800.** Or you may access our World Wide Web site on the Internet at **www.hazelden.org.**